# art out of agony

## The Holocaust Theme in Literature, Sculpture and Film

**CBC Enterprises/les Entreprises Radio-Canada**

MONTRÉAL • TORONTO • NEW YORK • LONDON

Published by CBC Enterprises/les Entreprises Radio-Canada, a division of the Canadian Broadcasting Corporation, P.O. Box 500, Station A, Toronto (Ontario), Canada M5W 1E6.

Publié par CBC Enterprises/les Entreprises Radio-Canada, une division de la Société Radio-Canada, C.P. 500, Succursale «A», Toronto (Ontario), Canada M5W 1E6.

**Canadian Cataloguing in Publication Data**

Lewis, Stephen, 1937-
   Art out of agony

Based on programs aired on the CBC radio series Stereo morning, from May 30-June 3, 1983.
Bibliography:
**ISBN 0-88794-121-4**

1. Holocaust, Jewish (1939-1945), in literature.
2. Holocaust, Jewish (1939-1945), in motion pictures.
I. Stereo morning (Radio program). II. Title.

PN56.H55148       809'93358       C83-098804-1

General Manager/Directeur général: Guy R. Mazzeo
Publisher/Éditeur: Glenn Edward Witmer
Editor/Révision: Ex Libris/Charis Wahl and Jennifer Glossop
Managing Editor/Direction de la rédaction: Robert Daley
Research/Recherches: Marilyn Powell and Kim Corveat
Designer/Conception graphique: Jorge Guastavino/Grafika Art Studios
Cover Photograph/Photo de la couverture: Allan Finkelman
Typesetter/Composition: CompuScreen Typesetting Limited
Printer/Impression: The Alger Press Limited

Distributed to the trade by:
Macmillan of Canada (a division of Gage Publishing Limited), Toronto

Printed and bound in Canada
1  2  3  4  5  6  7  8  9  /  92  91  90  89  88  87  86  85  84

# Contents

*The CBC-FM programme on which this book is based was the 1983 winner of a special* **Media Human Rights Award** *from the League for Human Rights of B'nai Brith Canada.*

# Acknowledgements

The publisher gratefully acknowledges permission to reprint passages from the following original works. Excerpts may be found on these pages:

13. *Tzili* by **Aharon Appelfeld** copyright © 1983 by Aharon Appelfeld and reprinted by permission of the publisher E.P. Dutton Inc. English translation copyright © 1983 by Dalya Bilu.

18. *The Age of Wonders* by **Aharon Appelfeld** copyright © 1982 by Aharon Appelfeld. English translation copyright © 1982 by Dalya Bilu. First published in Canada in 1982 by Lester and Orpen Dennys Limited. Reprinted with permission.

20. *Badenheim 1939* by **Aharon Appelfeld** copyright © 1980 by Aharon Appelfeld. English translation copyright © 1980 by Dalya Bilu. Reprinted with permission.

32, 36 and 43. *Hasidic Tales of the Holocaust* by **Yaffa Eliach** reprinted by permission of Russell and Volkening, Inc. as agents for the author. Copyright © 1982 by Yaffa Eliach.

57 and 66. *The Portage to San Cristòbal of A.H.* by **George Steiner** copyright © 1979 and 1981 by George Steiner. Reprinted by permission of Simon & Schuster, Inc.

73 and 86. *The White Hotel* by **D.M. Thomas** copyright © 1981 by Victor Gollancz. Reprinted with permission.

94 and 103 *Jacob The Liar* by **Jurek Becker** copyright © 1969 by Aufbau-Verlag, Berlin and Weimar. Reissued by Suhrkamp Verlag, Frankfurt. All rights reserved. English translation copyright © 1975 by Harcourt Brace Jovanovich, Inc. Reprinted by permission of the publisher.

161. *Night* by **Elie Wiesel** reprinted by permission of Hill and Wang (now a division of Farrar, Straus and Giroux, Inc.). Copyright © 1958 by Editions De Minuit. English translation copyright © 1960 by MacGibbon and Kee.

174, 176 and 180. *Sophie's Choice* by **William Styron** reprinted by permission of Don Congdon Associates, Inc. Copyright © 1976, 1978 and 1979 by William Styron.

Grateful acknowledgement is made to the Toronto Jewish Congress Holocaust Remembrance Committee for the use of "*A Selected Bibliography on the Holocaust*," prepared by Jill Hertzman and Alan Bardikoff.

The cover photograph of "*The Holocaust*" sculpted by George Segal is reproduced courtesy of the Sidney Janis Gallery.

The CBC Stereo Morning programme, "*Art and The Holocaust*," on which this material is based, was produced in 1983. The Executive Producer was Anne Gibson and the Producer was Marilyn Powell.

# Foreword

It was Marilyn Powell of CBC-FM's *Stereo Morning* who first approached me to consider this project. I was simultaneously flattered and apprehensive, but mostly apprehensive. It seemed overwhelming for three reasons.

First, the subject matter. I'm a Jew who lived half of his life in a way best described as nominally Jewish. I was saved from a passive assimilation by marriage alone.

I wasn't oblivious to the world around me—ours was an active socialist and internationalist family—but, partly because of these other preoccupations, the Holocaust impinged only indirectly on my life, and as fate would have it, I—unlike most Jews of my age—cannot name even a distant relative whose life was extinguished in the death camps.

In such circumstances, one grows up knowing, of course, about the Holocaust, but only reconnoitring its horrors, never confronting its emotional devastation directly. This series of interviews was, therefore, my first total immersion and a desperately painful experience. I have utterly no regrets; I should have come to grips with it years ago. But you can imagine my apprehensions at the outset.

Second, the artistic format. I have spent most of my adult life in politics, being interviewed, almost never interviewing. There develops a careless egocentricity; an assumption that one exists to give answers, not to ask questions. I'm embarrassed by that, but it must be admitted. And I think that the interviews in this book suffer from my lack of skill as interlocutor.

Third, the subjects themselves. Novelists, critics, artists and film-makers are not intrinsically intimidating, but I was helplessly unfamiliar with their works, and had to undertake my own crash course in Holocaust literature, art and film. My field of study was history, so I approached the task at hand with an epic reservoir of ignorance. I know that it shows; I hope that it does not impede.

Yet, whatever inadequacies intrude, it seems to me that the project was worthwhile, and I'm immensely gratified to have been associated with it.

From the writers and artists in this book there flows a memorable wisdom about the most horrific episode in human history. As they struggle, through literature, art and film to plumb the nature of evil, to illumine the anguish of victim and survivor, and to cope with the insanity of the final solution, we, the readers and observers, begin faintly to understand. And while it will never be possible to understand fully, it is desperately important that all of us at least wrestle with the reasons for the descent into barbarism, and attempt to confront its results.

This is, alas, a world where anti-Semitism still flourishes. Even now, shielded by the protective comfort of democracy, ugly racist spasms occur, whether in Eckville, Alberta or Paris, France. A civilized society can never defend to excess the rights of its minorities. New generations must be made aware of the nightmares of the past, and how they connect, organically, with the destructive impulses of the present. And they must be made aware while the survivors of the Holocaust are still alive.

If this little book achieves even a particle of that, then it and the radio series are in every way justified.

As in all such undertakings, the role of the interviewer is greatly enhanced by others. I must thank for both courage and insight, Anne Gibson, the executive producer of *Stereo Morning*, whose idea the entire project was. Without the help of my wife, Michele Landsberg, and my good friend, Ellen Charney, I would never have been able to conduct several of the conversations at all. The tortured unedited transcripts were brought into shape by Charis Wahl and Jennifer Glossop. Terry Campbell gave me a running perspective as we talked, on air, about the interviews and their meaning. But above all, it was Marilyn Powell who shaped this undertaking, nurturing it with intelligence, insight and scrupulous care. Indeed, it is to Marilyn to whom the achievement, if any, primarily belongs.

**Stephen Lewis**
*September, 1983*

# Aharon
# Appelfeld

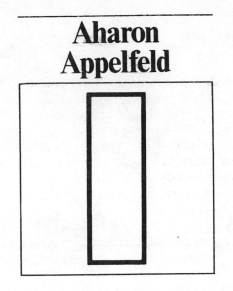

JUDITH APPELFELD

Aharon Appelfeld was born in 1932 in Czernovitz, in the Bukovina region of Romania. During the Nazi invasion of the area, he was captured and deported to a labour camp, from which he escaped when he was eight years old. Until he was eleven he lived off the land, wandering about the forests. Then he was picked up by the Red Army and put to work in army camps throughout the Ukraine. Eventually he wandered to Italy and, finally, arrived safely in Palestine.

He is a teacher of Hebrew literature at Ben Gurion University in Beersheba, Israel. His novels, both in the original Hebrew and in translation, have earned him universal acclaim from the critics for their power to evoke images of unspeakable horror through masterfully controlled prose. Three of his twenty novels have been translated into English: *Badenheim 1939*, *The Age of Wonders*, and *Tzili: The Story of a Life*.

Aharon Appelfeld is married and has three children.

Aharon Appelfeld was one of the sweetest, gentlest, and most thoughtful of the people whom I interviewed. Unhappily, because of his discomfort in the English language, his words seem a little halting and his ideas a little abrupt.

But the truth of the matter is that Appelfeld's novels are magnificent. More than any other contemporary writer, he catches, unerringly, the nature of assimilated European Jewish society on the eve of the Holocaust, and somehow takes his readers through the chill of enveloping horror without ever wallowing in the horror itself. *The Age of Wonders* is the finest book I have read in the genre of Holocaust literature.

---

*Mr. Appelfeld, you have, I believe, written a memoir of your own experiences in the war years.*

I have never written a memoir. I was a child, as you know, in the war time. I was eight years old when World War Two broke out. I remember all the events, but it is not a chronological memory; rather it is an inner memory, a secret memory.

*Is it fair to say that the character Tzili, in your novel of the same name, is in some respects an extension of those memories?*

Yes, she is. I wanted to give an objective dimension to my life, to the fate of the Jewish people. So I needed a kind of objectivisation of the subject.

They walked along the riverside, toward the south. The sun shone on the green fields. Now it seemed that Zigi Baum was floating on the current, his arms outspread. Every now and then his image was reflected on the surface of the water. No one stopped to gaze at this shining reflection. The current widened as it approached the dam, a mighty torrent of water.

Later on a few people turned off to the right. They turned

off together, without asking any questions or saying good-by. Tzili watched them walk away. They showed no signs of anger or of happiness. They went on walking at the same pace—for some reason, in another direction.

Tzili, it appeared, was already in the sixth month of her pregnancy. Her belly was taut and heavy but her legs, despite the difficulties of the road, walked without stumbling. When the refugees stopped to rest, they ate in silence. The strange disappearance of Zigi Baum had infected them with a subtle terror, unlike anything they had experienced before.

Tzili was happy. Not a happiness which had any outward manifestations: the fetus stirring inside her gave her an appetite and a lust for life. Not so the others: death clung even to their clothes. They tried to shake it off by walking.

From time to time they quickened their pace and Tzili fell behind. They were as absorbed in themselves now as they had been before in their card game. No one asked: "Where is she?" but nevertheless Tzili felt that their closeness to her was stronger than their distraction. . . .

Once, when they had stopped to rest, a woman asked her: "Isn't it hard for you?"

"No," said Tzili simply.

"And do you want the baby?"

"Yes."

The woman was surprised by Tzili's reply. She looked at her as if she were some stupid, senseless creature. Then she was sorry and her expression changed to one of wonder and pity: "How will you bring it up?"

"I'll keep it with me all the time," said Tzili simply.

Tzili too wanted to ask: "Where are you from?" But she had learned not to ask. On their last halt a quarrel had broken out between two women as a result of a tactless question. People were very tense and questions brought their repressed anger seething to the surface.

"How old are you?" asked the woman.

"Fifteen."

"So young." Wonder softened the woman's face.

Tzili offered her a piece of bread and she said, "Thank you."

"I," said the woman, "have lost my children. It seems to me

that I did everything I could, but they were lost anyway. The oldest was nine and the youngest seven. And I am alive, as you see, even eating. Me they didn't harm. I must be made of iron."

A pain shot through Tzili's diaphragm and she closed her eyes.

"Don't you feel well?" asked the woman.

"It'll pass," said Tzili.

"Give me your mug and I'll fetch you some water."

When the woman returned Tzili was already sitting calmly on the ground. The woman raised the cup to Tzili's mouth and Tzili drank. The woman now wanted more than anything to help Tzili, but she did not know how. Tzili, in spite of everything, had more food than she did.

Straight after this night fell and the woman sank to the ground and slept. She shrank to the size of a child of six. Tzili wanted to cover the woman with her tattered coat, but she immediately suppressed this impulse. She did not want to frighten her.

The others were awake but passive. The isolated words which fluttered in the air were as inward as a conversation between two lovers, no longer young.

The night was warm and fine and Tzili remembered the little yard at home, where she had spent so many hours. Every now and then her mother would call, "Tzili," and Tzili would reply, "Here I am." Of her entire childhood, only this was left. All the rest was shrouded in a heavy mist. She was seized by longing for the little yard. As if it were the misty edge of the Garden of Eden.

"I have to eat." She banished the vision and immediately put her hand into the haversack and tore off a piece of bread. The bread was dry. A few grains of coal were embedded in its bottom crust. She liked the taste of the bread. Afterward she ate a little smoked meat. With every bite she felt her hunger dulled.\*

*Your works are obviously pre-occupied with the Holocaust theme. Do you feel that you will write about other things? Or are you driven to write of the Holocaust?*

---

\*See Acknowledgements page for all excerpt sources

It was essential in my life. I spent my childhood in Europe from 1940 to 1946. That time shaped my life and shaped my way of thinking, my way of feeling, my way of reacting. It shaped my generation. It is central in Jewish history, so I cannot escape it.

*And yet you find it difficult to deal with directly.*

I would say that, artistically, it is impossible to deal with it directly. It's like the sun. You cannot look at the sun; the temperature is too high. The Holocaust is a kind of temperature you cannot speak, you cannot utter, you cannot feel. You have to degradate it to an extent in order to speak of it.

*Irving Howe wrote a wonderful review of* Badenheim 1939 *in which he says: "Only a very small number of writers have managed to evoke imaginatively the inner strains of the Holocaust, and they, through some deep unlocated intuition, approach it obliquely, furtively. They seem to feel that the unspeakable is beyond direct representation, perhaps even that it is a presumption to try directly to represent it." I take it that reflects your view?*

Yes. The unspeakable is a secret. You can only surround it. You cannot speak about it. It is like death. We will never know what death really means. We know it before and after, and we can guess, we can try to feel, try to understand, but we'll never understand it.

*Is it only a survivor who can write as you write about the Holocaust?*

I cannot imagine, except by a miracle, someone writing about the Holocaust who was not a part of it.

*Not even a Jew?*

Not even a Jew, no. Sometimes writers use it as a vehicle, but it is terrible to use it as a vehicle, as a psychological vehicle, or as a motive in a novel.

Fiction, by its very nature, is intimacy, and to write about the Holocaust means to be a part of the Jewish fate, of Jewish history, to be a part of the Jewish mythology in the broad meaning of the word. I appreciate some experiments, but that is what I would call them—experiments.

*Writers can never touch the truth unless they are part of the Jewish experience?*

I guess so, but you know there are miracles. There are always miracles. But to write about the Holocaust means to be very close to it, to be a part of it, to be deeply involved in it, not only as in an abstract idea, but as a deep feeling, an inner feeling. Writers try to understand traumatic events. I can understand the attempt, but I am afraid that the result will not be authentic. It will be superficial or misleading or false.

*Or exploitative.*

Or exploitative, yes. That is the most dangerous. A deep experience is like a deep pain; you have to be very careful dealing with it.

*And yet suddenly, Mr. Appelfeld, there is a profusion of novels and films and television programmes that deal with the Holocaust. Why at this moment in time?*

Because the Holocaust is still a cloud, a heavy, dark cloud over our heads, as Jews, as non-Jews. People try to explain it positively, try to understand, try to be close to it. Jews who have not experienced it, those in America or Canada, try to identify themselves with it. I can understand this desire, but I am afraid of it. The Holocaust was such an extraordinary event that people who have not been into that fire, that terrible fire, would not understand, or would simplify it or vulgarize it. That is the danger: vulgarization of this delicate matter.

*Mr. Appelfeld, the picture your books paint of the nature of Jewish society in the pre-World-War-Two days is not a very flattering one.*

He was totally absorbed in his fantasies about the Baroness von Drück: the revival of Austrian literature, journals, books, a popular library to fight the evil spirits of the time.

And thus, without anything being decided, heavy days came upon us, days charged with moisture, the days before a storm. No one imagined that the storm was already on its way. The autumn light was in its full beauty, cold and clear, the businessmen came and went, and Mother did not forgo a single visit to the charitable institutions that still remained open. She kept a strict timetable. There was no cash left in the house, but there were still plenty of clothes.

How ignorant we were of the approaching end the following facts will testify: Father prepared himself to go to Vienna and help the Baroness von Drück revive her literary salon, Mother labored to set up a new home for the paralyzed and a soup kitchen for tramps. They quarreled ceaselessly. There was nothing about which they were in agreement. The polite, delicate silence that had once reigned in our house was broken into bits. The smell of mothballs and moldy old books filled the rooms with an autumnal suffocation. No one cared any more about anyone else's feelings. Helga was miserable without her front teeth. She kept her nose in her books and studied until late at night. But her efforts bore no fruit. Now too her grades were humiliating. I did well at school, but nobody praised me for anything, as if it were taken for granted that I had to excel, or at least hold my own.

Since nobody knew that these were the last days in this house, on this street, and behind the grid of this lattice, which continued to cast its damp shade on the pavement, since nobody knew, everyone buried himself in his own affairs as if there were no end to this life. Father kept his literary delusions to which he continued to cling even when everything teetered on the edge of the abyss. He kept on writing and rewriting sentences and paragraphs, as if they were not words written on a page but crimes that could not be left unpunished. Mother too showed herself no mercy. From morning till night she worked, and in the evenings she would sit with Helga over her homework. Nobody cared now about anybody else's feelings.

It's not flattering because it was an assimilated society, and assimilation, by its very nature, is not flattering. The assimilated Jews were denying themselves. They were denying their identity. They were trying to escape from themselves. That is psychologically a dangerous process and culturally an ugly process.

*You were quite unsparing in your portraits of Bruno's father in the novel* The Age of Wonders *and of Tzili's parents in* Tzili.

They were the assimilated Jews who escaped from their sources, from their culture. For the Austrian Jews, the Ostjuden—the East European Jews—were a symbol of a primitive, ugly, non-cultured, superstitious, anachronistic society.

*Were they like that?*

No, they were the opposite. East European Jewry had a very rich culture, full of life, authentic life. But to the assimilated Jews, East European Jewry was primitive, very unacceptable. They hated them. They could not accept them. But, you see, I'm not judging the people. Even in my book, *The Age of Wonders*, I'm not judging people. A writer tries to make an effort to understand. I do not divide people into good and bad. I just try to understand them, even the assimilated Jew, whom I do not identify with. I still try to understand the route of assimilation, the route of escaping from himself. It is a very old Jewish tragedy to escape from yourself, not to be you, to be something else. Very old, and it exists all throughout the Jewish tradition.

*I sometimes wanted to ask, as I read your book, Mr. Appelfeld, where was the left wing? Where were the Zionists? Where were the activists, those who weren't prone to succumbing to the seduction of non-Jewish society?*

We have to understand that the main tendency of the twentieth-century Jew was to become a universalist. Even the Zionist movement was a universalist movement. Then the Holocaust came and forced them to become Jews, to become Jews physically. You were a Jew because your mother was Jewish, and it didn't matter if you were a believer, if you were a Communist or a Bundist. The blood in your body was condemning you. And this was a tragedy, a terrible tragedy for these people.

From the station they could still see Badenheim: a low hill cut like a cone, with the roofs of the houses like little pieces of folded cardboard. Only the hotel and bell tower seemed real. The kiosk owner was delighted to see all the people, and their eyes lit up at the sight of the lemonade, the newspapers, and journals—a testimony to the life that was still going on around them. Dr. Langmann bought the financial weekly and studied it like a man returning to a beloved city after years of absence.
The musicians crowded together in a corner, in the shade. Some of the plates had been broken on the way, and they had to unpack their cases and pack them again. This annoying necessity, which gave rise to anger and mutual recriminations, marred the festive atmosphere a little. From here the carriages would pick the people up and there was always the same fragrance in the air, the fragrance of the transition from the town to the country, and from the station to the enchanted Badenheim. There were no carriages now, but the fragrance still lingered in the air, mingled with an intoxicating dampness.
And suddenly the sky opened and light broke out of the heavens. The valley in all its glory and the hills scattered about

filled with the abundance, and even the trembling, leafless trees standing wretchedly at the edge of the station seemed to breathe a sigh of relief.

'What did I tell you?' exclaimed Dr. Pappenheim, opening his arms in an expansive gesture that seemed too big for him. Tears of joy came into his eyes. All the misery of the days in confinement suddenly burst inside him.

The light poured from the low hills directly onto the station platform. There was nowhere to hide. 'Come and see, everybody!' Mitzi suddenly cried, in an affected feminine voice. A little distance away, as if on an illuminated tray, a man was walking with two armed policemen behind him. They came closer as if they were being borne on the light.

'Peter, Peter!' shouted the hotel owner in relief.

Peter.

But their amazement was cut short. An engine, an engine coupled to four filthy freight cars, emerged from the hills and stopped at the station. Its appearance was as sudden as if it had risen from a pit in the ground. 'Get in!' yelled invisible voices. And the people were sucked in. Even those who were standing with a bottle of lemonade in their hands, a bar of chocolate, the headwaiter with his dog—they were all sucked in as easily as grains of wheat poured into a funnel. Nevertheless Dr. Pappenheim found time to make the following remark: 'If the coaches are so dirty it must mean that we have not far to go.'

*So their Jewishness gained definition against the Holocaust?*

Yes. I grew up in a very assimilated Jewish family. I became Jewish. I would call myself a deeply involved Jew and an active Jew. It was mainly through the Holocaust. I suffered. My body became Jewish, and through my body I became a Jew. The suffering of my body suddenly caused me to think about my Jewishness, about the past, about my parents, about Jewish faith and history, and so on. It's unpleasant, tragic; but it happened to a lot of Jews in America, and probably in Canada and Israel.

*This sense of self-definition that was born in the Holocaust was subsequently defined in Israel. Do you agree that Israel is the second part of the process by which Jews have achieved a self-definition?*

You mean that in a positive way?

*Yes, in a positive way.*

Yes, I agree, but still, you know, even in Israel, it's a question of the crystallization of Jewish feelings. In the Zionist movement were two deep tendencies. One tendency said, let me escape from Jewish fate and become a part of world history; and another tendency said, let us become Jews, let us become full Jews. And these two strong tendencies still need crystallization.

*Mr. Appelfeld, running through your books is an emphasis on academic excellence and learning.*

Yes. Learning was an obsession to the Jews for two reasons. First, because Jewish religion is not contemplation, but a kind of permanent studying. This is really the mythological source of the obsession. Then, in modern times, learning became for Jews a kind of an obsession to be better, to be the best. You can see it even in America.

*Is that why in* Tzili *the survivor, who was an engineer, wants to pick up exactly where he left off and go and complete his degree? Even after the intervening Holocaust years, study is central to his life?*

Yes, yes. How tragic it is! He has even forgotten that there was a Holocaust. You see how the obsession to become an engineer or a lawyer takes over? Yes, it's a very strong Jewish obsession to have a degree.

*And you would say that that continues to be true?*

Yes, studying, learning, an obsessive matter in Jewish history, is an issue, a serious issue, up to modern time.

*And it was, I take it, a distracting issue in pre-war Jewry, distracting in the sense that it obsessed Jews to the extent that it made them impervious to what was happening around them.*

Yes, but by trying to become a positive part of Western civilization, they forgot that, in the eyes of Christian mythology, they were still Jews.

*What about Franz Kafka, Mr. Appelfeld? He is not only very special to the academic father in* The Age of Wonders, *but, I gather, special to you?*

Kafka is close to me, first of all, because he is a Jewish writer, even though Jews are not mentioned in his novels and short stories, only in his diaries. He is also very close to me because he has some Talmudical qualities in his writing, which I appreciate very much. I would say he is probably the deepest Jewish writer we have.

*When you say a Jewish writer, what do you mean, more specifically?*

Born in a Jewish family, writing in a Jewish language, rooted in Jewish mythology, identifying himself with the Jewish faith.

*How do you apply that to Kafka?*

Kafka miraculously absorbed Jewish contents. I do not know how to explain it, but he absorbed it. Very strange.

*Irving Howe quotes you as saying, "Help came unexpectedly from Franz Kafka the Jew. To look at* The Trial *was to feel that he had been with us wherever we had been. Every line of that book spoke of us. In his language we found suspicion and doubt, but also the sick longing for an explanation." Does that remain true for the current survivors of the Holocaust?*

I would say for the intelligentsia it is a truth, yes. On one side there was scepticism and suspicion, but on the other side there was a deep yearning for meaning, because people who survived the Holocaust have a desire—a deep desire among the intelligentsia mainly—to give meaning to life, to find a meaning.

*The survivors I know and have read say that one of the reasons for surviving was to tell the world what happened. And yet at the end of Tzili you convey a sense of bleakness. It's as though their testament is somehow muted by sadness.*

You know, after great events, after traumatic events, we remain dumb, wordless, and that is really one of the tragedies of the Holocaust. The Holocaust made us dumb, wordless. That is a kind of deep truth that I wanted to convey through *Tzili.*

*What happened to the survivors? Can the feelings of the survivors be put in rational terms?*

We, as human beings, try to rationalize. It is very human; it is one of our weaknesses to rationalize, and we do it very often. And after the Holocaust, people tried to rationalize their feelings, but what is typical of people who survived the Holocaust is that they mainly concealed their feelings and did not speak about them. We have a generation of people who survived the Holocaust and concealed their feelings because they were untransmittable.

*Are the survivors destined to spend their lives exorcising the sense of guilt, the sense that they shouldn't even be alive, that they left people behind? There are very deep feelings of that in* Tzili.

I'm dealing with human beings, not abstract form. You feel guilt, but the next day you forget about your guilt and you are eating and you are dreaming and you are loving and you are hating. That is the way people react, and it is a very deep truth even in Jewish life. Every one of us is a Jew after the Holocaust. We had a good lesson, but still we continue to be assimilated Jews, escaping from ourselves. We still forget. That is a fact of life.

*When Bruno in* The Age of Wonders *returns to seek the explanation of all that had happened, the community he meets, the encounters he has are every bit as random and anarchical and anti-Semitic as before. There is a great bleakness in that. Are you saying, through the power of the novel, that there is no hope, or that the hope is muted, or that it can happen again?*

I'm not a politician. I'm not a prophet. I'm not a theologian. And I'm not going to predict what's going to happen. I speak mainly about deep Jewish fears, deep Jewish intuitions. Let us hope that these will be meaningless fears, but it is a very deep Jewish fear that this story doesn't have an end, that the suffering is somewhere continuing, that the Jew is still demonised in different parts of the world, is still accepted as a demon of Western civilization. I believe that Jewish experience applies to every human being in the world, because it is a deep experience, a strange experience, and a painful experience, but an experience that deserves to be known.

# Yaffa Eliach

Story-teller, poet, playwright and historian Yaffa Eliach was born in Vilna, Poland. She spent much of her early years in hiding from the Nazis. After the war her mother was murdered in a pogrom and her father exiled by the Russians to a work camp in the Gulag. An uncle took her to Israel and moved to the United States in 1954.

After receiving her doctorate from the City University of New York, she taught both elementary and high school. Today, Eliach is Professor of History and Literature in the Department of Judaic Studies at Brooklyn College, and Director of the Center for Holocaust Studies. Even before the great critical and popular success of *Hasidic Tales of the Holocaust*, Eliach's historical research into the origins of the Hasidic movement and the Holocaust brought her a wide radio, television and public lecture audience as well as academic recognition.

Yaffa Eliach and her husband live in New York. They have two children.

I wish that the reader could hear Yaffa Eliach's vibrant voice behind her words. She speaks with a caring persuasive urgency, the tone and cadence almost Hasidic in their rhythms. There is something wonderfully touching and wise about Yaffa Eliach; never a moment's guile, never a false note—one trusts every word. I treasured my conversation with her and would have liked it to go on much longer.

---

*Can you explain the Hasidic tradition of story-telling?*

One of the major contributions of the Hasidic movement was story-telling. It was so paramount to the movement that the founder, Israel Baal Shem Tov, who died in 1760, felt that story-telling could restore all lines of communication between men and men, and men and God. When everything else fails, the only resort left to man is to tell a story, a tale. It has the power to mend, to restore. At a later time, the rabbi of Rizhin stated that a time will come when society will reach its lowest ebb of humanity, and nothing will be able to elevate it and restore it to a better position. The only medium left to mankind will be telling a story.

*Was it also deeply religious?*

Strangely enough, the Hasidic tale does not have to be deeply religious. The Hasidic tradition tells us that if a man goes to the market place and he hears a good story and he feels he can utilize this story in order to bring out compassion or love for his fellow man, he should adopt that story. The source is immaterial. So the sources of the Hasidic tale do not all stem from the religious tradition, although they are utilized by the religious story-teller.

*How early were Hasidic stories published?*

The first collection of Hasidic stories was printed in 1806. They were the collected tales told by Rabbi Nachman of Brazlav, the great-grandson of the founder of the Hasidic movement. He was born in 1772 and died in 1810. Since then there have been many books written about Hasidic tales; but in the last hundred years, there were no new Hasidic tales, they were old tales retold by new story-tellers. My collection is unique in that they are new tales, and obviously told by a new story-teller. It is the first collection ever to be told by a woman. All Hasidic story-tellers were men.

*What drove you to assemble the collection of tales?*

I was teaching, and still am, in Brooklyn College. We were one of the first campuses in the United States to introduce Holocaust studies, and there was a sense of despair, I felt, in my classroom. I wanted material that somehow would not modify realities, but would be an expression not only of man's inhumanity to man, but of the greatness of man's spirit even in the valley of death. I started to interview Holocaust survivors. Since the campus is in Brooklyn, in the midst of the largest Hasidic community in the world, it was natural that some of the tales that emerged in my interviews were Hasidic tales. It was then that I felt that the Hasidic tale would help me to convey to my students the message that man is basically good—there is hope for mankind, evil is transient—and, indeed, to use the Hasidic tradition to modify or to create a buffer between us and the terrible events of the Holocaust, and yet be faithful, at the same time, to the Holocaust. It was quite a task for me to be faithful to the original story-teller. Many times I was dealing with eleven languages. I tried to convey the structure of the sentence that was told to me either in Hebrew or Yiddish or Polish or Russian, to maintain the flavour of the Hasidic tale, and yet write it in English. This transformation from one language to another language while remaining faithful to a certain structure and to the voice of the story-teller was quite a task in itself.

*And English is not a language of horror, is it?*

No, it's not. It's not even a language of sorrow. There were so many words used to express sorrow in the original tales that I felt, at times, at a loss for words in English. It's not only the horror, it's also the sorrow. Russian is great for sorrow!

*Did you, as a survivor, regard it as a personal testament?*

Strangely enough, no. I was seven when I was liberated. There is that urge to tell, but there is also that great urge to listen to the stories that others have to tell, to let them be the witness. I would rather be the listener, the listener who retells their stories. I did not view myself as a survivor, and I don't even now. While I was in hiding during World War Two, I learned to listen, being among adults. Not having a present or a past to share, we were denied our childhood. It was the constant listening to the adults speak about the miraculous days when they were young and were playing outdoors that I think conditioned me as an interviewer.

*The tales walk that line between reality and unreality—I gather there was a monumental job involved in verification.*

For me it was very important not to leave the Hasidic tale as just a Hasidic tale. Since I was trained as an historian (as a matter of fact my dissertation was on the origins of the Hasidic movement and its emergence in Russia and in the Ukraine), I felt a great need to satisfy the students of history. Each tale, as much as possible, had to be authenticated because I wanted it to become not only a tale but, if possible, a document.

*Most of the stories were about absolutely real events, were they not?*

All the stories are about real events. It was important to me to describe the event the way it took place. If a person told me there was a selection on a certain date, and that this happened to him, I recorded the story the way he told it to me, and then checked out the event in supporting material. If I could not find the verification, I did not include it in my book. So all the tales are indeed events that did take place.

## Hovering above the Pit

It was a dark, cold night in the Janowska Road camp. Suddenly, a stentorian shout pierced the air: "You are all to evacuate the barracks immediately and report to the vacant lot. Anyone remaining inside will be shot on the spot!"

Pandemonium broke out in the barracks. People pushed their way to the doors while screaming the names of friends and relatives. In a panic-stricken stampede, the prisoners ran in the direction of the big open field.

Exhausted, trying to catch their breath, they reached the field. In the middle were two huge pits.

Suddenly, with their last drop of energy, the inmates realized where they were rushing, on that cursed dark night in Janowska.

Once more, the cold, healthy voice roared in the night: "Each of you dogs who values his miserable life and wants to cling to it must jump over one of the pits and land on the other side. Those who miss will get what they rightfully deserve—ra-ta-ta-ta-ta."

Imitating the sound of a machine gun, the voice trailed off into the night followed by a wild, coarse laughter. It was clear to the inmates that they would all end up in the pits. Even at the best of times it would have been impossible to jump over them, all the more so on that cold dark night in Janowska. The prisoners standing at the edge of the pits were skeletons, feverish from disease and starvation, exhausted from slave labor and sleepless nights. Though the challenge that had been given them was a matter of life and death, they knew that for the S.S. and the Ukrainian guards it was merely another devilish game.

Among the thousands of Jews on that field in Janowska was the Rabbi of Bluzhov, Rabbi Israel Spira. He was standing with a friend, a freethinker from a large Polish town whom the rabbi had met in the camp. A deep friendship had developed between the two.

"Spira, all of our efforts to jump over the pits are in vain. We only entertain the Germans and their collaborators, the Askaris. Let's sit down in the pits and wait for the bullets to end our wretched existence," said the friend to the rabbi.

"My friend," said the rabbi, as they were walking in the direction of the pits, "man must obey the will of God. If it was decreed from heaven that pits be dug and we be commanded to jump, pits will be dug and jump we must. And if, God forbid, we fail and fall into the pits, we will reach the World of Truth a second later, after our attempt. So, my friend, we must jump."

The rabbi and his friend were nearing the edge of the pits; the pits were rapidly filling up with bodies.

The rabbi glanced down at his feet, the swollen feet of a fifty-three-year-old Jew ridden with starvation and disease. He looked at his young friend, a skeleton with burning eyes.

As they reached the pit, the rabbi closed his eyes and commanded in a powerful whisper, "We are jumping!" When they opened their eyes, they found themselves standing on the other side of the pit.

"Spira, we are here, we are here, we are alive!" the friend repeated over and over again, while warm tears streamed from his eyes. "Spira, for your sake, I am alive; indeed, there must be a God in heaven. Tell me, Rebbe, how did you do it?"

"I was holding on to my ancestral merit. I was holding on to the coattails of my father, and my grandfather and my great-grandfather, of blessed memory," said the rabbi and his eyes searched the black skies above. "Tell me, my friend, how did you reach the other side of the pit?"

"I was holding on to you," replied the rabbi's friend.

*Let us take the first tale, the magnificent story "Hovering above the Pit." As I recall, Rabbi Israel Spira finds himself transported across the death pit by his ancestral ties and his friend is transported by hanging on to the rabbi. Now maybe it's just my hopeless banality, but that is not a real event.*

No, it is a real event.

A friend of mine was in another concentration camp. She escaped during a death march. About twenty policemen were chasing her. She was eighteen at the time and wore only clogs. And yet she ran so fast that twenty policemen, well dressed in warm winter uniforms and boots, could not catch this starved, emaciated youngster. So I think that, according to the perception of the rabbi, he indeed spanned those huge graves in Janowska. When he told me this story, he showed me the street where he lived in Brooklyn, and he said, you see this street? Four cars can pass and yet this is how large that grave was in Janowska. Of course, one can speculate and find all kinds of logical answers, but I was so impressed with his faith, even forty years later, that I recorded it in the way he told me. I spent three months at libraries looking for pictures of the graves in Janowska, and I did find them eventually.

*The book is meant, I take it, to convey a sense of hope, even at the nadir of despair. Is that fair?*

Yes, it's very fair, but if I may add, it's more than hope. It's faith in man's spirit, faith that no matter how difficult conditions are, no matter how we are humiliated—deprived of our own flesh, of our name, of our hair, of our friends, of our mothers, of our fathers—man's spirit still can overcome. It's a testimony to the spirit of humanity in the most inhuman place. And that's what attracted me: that spirit that cannot be conquered, that cannot be diminished; it will eventually overcome. So it's more than hope. It's faith in the strength of a human being.

*I was deeply moved by the stories but I was also oppressed by the random, capricious nature of survival. Even the most courageous human beings were still subject to a selection so arbitrary, so unpredictable, so quixotic, that it leaves one depressed in the reading.*

And yet all those who survived at one point *did* something; they somehow participated in that process. They did something. If they had remained passive they would not take the initiative, no matter what that initiative was. At times it was not their own; at times it was the man who was in the selection line behind them; at times the mother who pushed her son away; at times the mother who sent a man with a big basket to look for her lost son along the railroad tracks. In all cases, somebody took the initiative at a very crucial moment. And it's very difficult for survivors to admit this, because then they admit that they did something and that others did not. When I ask survivors, "To what do you attribute your survival?" they will never say, "It was because I ran fast." They will always say, "Well, it was chance, luck. I happened to be at the right place at the right time." Or they will use the Yiddish word *"bashert,"* "it was destined." I don't have a single tale in the book where the person did not take some sort of initiative.

*Even though the person could not foretell at the moment of the initiative what the consequences would be. . . .*

Yes. Many times, when I interviewed the person and listened to the tale, the person would tell me, at the very beginning, "Well, I didn't do anything in order to survive," and ten minutes later there would come an event in his story of survival that made a difference between being or not being.

*I gather that among the tales that are your favourites you have a great feeling for the story that begins the second part of the book, "Good Morning, Herr Müller." Can you explain why?*

# Good Morning,
# Herr Müller

Near the city of Danzig lived a well-to-do Hasidic rabbi, scion of prominent Hasidic dynasties. Dressed in a tailored black suit, wearing a top hat, and carrying a silver walking cane, the rabbi would take his daily morning stroll, accompanied by his tall, handsome son-in-law. During his morning walk it was the rabbi's custom to greet every man, woman, and child whom he met on his way with a warm smile and a cordial "Good morning." Over the years the rabbi became acquainted with many of his fellow townspeople this way and would always greet them by their proper title and name.

Near the outskirts of town, in the fields, he would exchange greetings with Herr Müller, a Polish *Volksdeutsche* (ethnic German). "Good morning, Herr Müller!" the rabbi would hasten to greet the man who worked in the fields. "Good morning, Herr Rabbiner!" would come the response with a good-natured smile.

Then the war began. The rabbi's strolls stopped abruptly. Herr Müller donned an S.S. uniform and disappeared from the fields. The fate of the rabbi was like that of much of the rest of Polish Jewry. He lost his family in the death camp of Treblinka and, after great suffering, was deported to Auschwitz.

One day, during a selection at Auschwitz, the rabbi stood on line with hundreds of other Jews awaiting the moment when their fates would be decided, for life or death. Dressed in a striped camp uniform, head and beard shaven and eyes feverish from starvation and disease, the rabbi looked like a walking skeleton. "Right! Left, left, left!" The voice in the distance drew nearer. Suddenly the rabbi had a great urge to see the face of the man with the snow-white gloves, small baton, and steely voice who played God and decided who should live and who should die. He lifted his eyes and heard his own voice speaking:

"Good morning, Herr Müller!"

"Good morning, Herr Rabbiner!" responded a human voice beneath the S.S. cap adorned with skull and bones. "What are you doing here?" A faint smile appeared on the rabbi's lips. The baton moved to the right—to life. The following day, the rabbi was transferred to a safer camp.

The rabbi, now in his eighties, told me in his gentle voice, "This is the power of a good-morning greeting. A man must always greet his fellow man."

I like it especially because I do not like to see the events of the Holocaust in black and white, good and evil. Even in Herr Müller, who was standing in line and selecting hundreds and maybe even thousands of people to send them to their deaths, there was a spark of humanity. He recognized a friend from pre-World War Two, and sent him to the right, which meant to life. I like that part because the process was so mechanized, so detached, that at times the Nazis and the SS are portrayed as mechanical soldiers. I look for the person in them. This frightens me, at the same time, because once you discover the person, you know that so many of us are capable of being in a uniform and making these strange decisions. If a man yields to a system and yet lapses into humanity for one single moment, that moment is important for me, because it makes him human.

*Do you then object to novels and films that use the executioner or victim theme in its ultimate extremes?*

I don't. I feel that in creating art—a film or a play or a book—there is a need to modify the reality. There is a need for an aesthetic distance. Personally, I feel at times that to describe the Holocaust in black and white, as all evil or all good, is not to place it within the historical process of civilization, of what we are all about. It's too easy, it's a very easy way out, to say it is all evil. We are not that way. The reader or the viewer, each of us should be on constant guard. How do I prevent my society, my government, my political system from falling into that trap, so that I will be able to uphold my convictions, my humanity?

*You use words like "aesthetic distance" as though it is never really possible to capture the event.*

The event was of such overwhelming magnitude that, in a way, it overpowered the imagination of an artist. Until the Holocaust, the artist always could create a horror that was greater than reality. He could describe hell; he could describe the most cruel events in the history of mankind. And yet they were created in the author's imagination. The Holocaust is that process in reverse. The imagination of the author is pale, is dwarfed, when compared to the magnitude and the size of the events themselves. Therefore, I selected events where the human spirit is very important, because personally I could not cope with events in which there is only the cruelty of men towards men, without those little buffer zones. That is why I selected the Hasidic tale, because it gave me the ability to work with the sparks in the darkness. Then I took it to art, to the form of the Hasidic tale, and then back to documentation. But if an artist works only with the artistic representation, the eye-witness will say that the description falls short of the reality that he witnessed. For the first time, art cannot match the reality that man created.

*That's exactly the position that Elie Wiesel takes when he deplores the fictionalizing of the events. He says that art cannot encompass it in that sense.*

I feel that we must make an attempt to capture it. Maybe it will fail, but we must make that attempt because, if we do not, we are admitting that our powers to destroy are greater than our powers to create. This is one victory I don't want to give to the Holocaust. Maybe our generation is not capable of it because the witnesses are here, the witnesses who hear and who smell the burning flesh, and who have constantly in front of their eyes that terrible planet of Auschwitz. And yet a generation will come when the witnesses will not be standing between the event and the portrayal of the event in art. Therefore, I think we must make attempts.

*But the artistic outpouring, which is prevalent now in*

*literature and film, is within the generation that still has the witnesses.*

Here we come to an additional aspect: the artist's responsibility. The artist who wants to come to terms with the Holocaust and makes an attempt—and I believe in many cases a very genuine one—must have a sense of self-restraint. There must be a responsibility not to distort the event. I don't speak only about recording it faithfully, but about being faithful to the historical reality. I think it is here that we transgress. We distort the realities: the political realities, the reality of the camps, the realities of the partisans. There is a distortion in art, and a distortion in history.

*May I take it from the abstract to the particular? How do* The White Hotel *and* Sophie's Choice *fit your description? Are they ultimately distortions, or was there restraint practised?*

From an artistic point of view, as a novel, *Sophie's Choice* is a well-structured southern novel, although the heroine is a Holocaust survivor. I do feel there is a measure of distortion. The ultimate victim, a Polish Catholic, suffers almost everything that was possible for a victim to suffer during the Holocaust. Many Polish individuals did suffer. However, I wonder, for instance, how many Catholic mothers stood on the platform in Auschwitz and had to make that selection that Sophie had to make. Well, hundreds of thousands of Jewish mothers had to make a choice as Sophie did. Yet I felt that the Jews in William Styron's novel are stereotyped. They are mostly not very positive characters.

*Are you saying that, fundamentally, for the sake of authenticity, a Jew has to write about the Holocaust?*

Oh, no. No way.

*Can you think of novels by non-Jews where the events have not been distorted?*

Yes: *This Way for the Gas, Ladies and Gentlemen*, by Polish writer Tadevsz Borowski. And quite a number of East European novelists. The events are described with great artistic force and intensity. You don't have to be Jewish; you have to be a good artist and be responsible.

*What do you think of the preoccupation in modern Germany with the Holocaust?*

I think, from the German movies that I have seen and the books I've read, that there is an attempt, as in many other countries occupied by the Germans, to emphasize their own tragedy rather than the suffering of the Jews—to emphasize that there were good Germans, that there were many people who suffered as much during the Holocaust as the Jews. Or the Jews are totally absent from the picture as the ultimate victim. There are a number of Hungarian movies, excellent movies, in which the thrust of the Holocaust is within the community of non-Jews. In the German movie *Das Boot*, "The Boat," there was a U-boat crew suffering. We felt quite sorry for the men and not so upset about the American or British sailors who were drowning just above in the waves of the ocean.

*Is it inevitable that ultimately the focus moves to the executioner, and the victim becomes almost a poignant relic?*

I am afraid that it may happen. Sometimes I have this fear that in the arts there will be a Holocaust without Jews. In the eighteen countries that were under German occupation, the people lived on the scarred landscape, so it is almost natural for them to populate that scarred landscape with their own heroes and heroines rather than with the Jews, who exist in only very small numbers in those countries. After a visit to Eastern Europe (I served on President Carter's Holocaust commission), I almost sensed, when I was walking in Poland and in Russia, that the ultimate victim was totally displaced. I was standing in Babi Yar. In my ears were ringing Yev-tushenko's words, both in Russian and in their English translation, and yet on the monument itself there is no mention whatsoever that Jews are buried there. And when I asked, the official response was, "Well, we don't make a distinction, as you do in the United States, between one ethnic group and another," which, of course, is not the case. I felt that there had been a double murder: first in fact, and then in memory. I just hope that artists will not become part of that partnership that is totally destroying the memory in movies, plays, novels, poetry. Yet it seems that this is the trend.

*I was struck, in the third section of the book, by the passion and anger that suffused the three or four episodes where you yourself were involved. We had gone through the whole book with you as raconteur and interpreter, and suddenly there you were yourself, leaping out at me from the pages with almost a cry of anguish, setting the record straight, as it were. Did you feel that way when you were doing it?*

When I was writing this book, there were difficult moments, moments when I felt I had been entrusted with this material. I worked on the book for seven years, in Israel and America, away from the scarred landscape. I was dealing with people who came here and were rebuilding their lives.

I had left Poland slowly, by train. Then I came back after so many years by plane. When the plane landed on Polish soil, I heard myself speak Polish. Here was a language that I used just for documents or translating what people said to me—I never, never spoke it. I heard myself saying words I had not spoken for maybe thirty-five, thirty-six years.

And suddenly there I was, back on that scarred land-scape, visiting Auschwitz, visiting the site of the Warsaw ghetto, travelling to Treblinka. I was clutching my American passport as if it were a pass to life. I almost insisted on getting a two-way ticket, coming and going, as a reassurance against the final destination. An enormous fear leapt at me from every corner.

A group of us from the president's commission came to Krakow directly from Auschwitz, and there we met the remnant of Polish Jewry, once the glory of the Jewry of the world. They were sitting there, old, in a group; they would not mingle with us. They were angry that members of the commission spoke English; they were angry that we came to their synagogue; they were angry that we came to Auschwitz. I asked one of them if there had been a marriage in the last few years in this synagogue, if a child had been circumcised in this synagogue, and he looked at me as if I came from another planet. It was then, in that synagogue, speaking to those people, that I sensed the enormity of the loss, the life that had been. It leaped at me from every corner.

I don't know if I broke cover in those stories, but the pain was overwhelming, even after I came back to the States. It took me months and months to get rid of that haunting fear. I almost was afraid to step on the ground in Treblinka; it was like stepping on bones, on blood. I was afraid that when the rains came, blood would fall from the sky. And yet there was sunshine, walls were rebuilt. But I kept hearing sounds and seeing sights of a different reality. You sensed it.

*Well, you broke cover with a kind of ambiguity. On the one hand you told the tales, and on the other you diminished the sense—forgive the use of the word—of hope. One felt from you such anger and anxiety and dismay and anguish that it was as though the Hasidic tales that preceded your own personal reflections were somehow more abstract.*

It is very interesting that you sensed it. I am not Hasidic. I come from a family that is opposed to the Hasidic movement. I am the first of my family in generations who married into a Hasidic family. My husband comes from the Hasidic tradition. I love that tradition because it gives me the ability to work out a difficult situation with hope and faith. And I hope that in the process some of it genuinely affects my own thoughts.

I am an optimistic person by nature. That's why I searched out the Hasidic tales. Yet there is definitely the pain of the Holocaust, the Lithuanian Jew in me, I suppose. With all that great hope, there is the pain, and the sense of loss, which cannot be diminished. There can be the hope for the future, but we have lost a whole centre of Jewish creativity. A young German artist walked over to me, near the Riema synagogue, and asked me to write a note for him, because he heard that if you place a note on the grave of the builder—one of the great minds of Polish Jewry who lived in the sixteenth century and built the synagogue in memory of his wife, who died at the age of twenty—it would bring success. I wrote that note for him. I really wanted this young artist to succeed; I wanted his posters to be on display in Frankfurt, and for him to win the award he wanted. There was no personal animosity. Again the teacher in me came out, or the mother in me, I don't know. I wanted this young man to be very successful. It didn't matter to me at that point that maybe his father or somebody in his family may have pointed the gun at my family. There was hope.

*And yet in the story almost immediately preceding, you tell of the young man who was in the Luftwaffe during the war.*

## The Telephone Operator

It was a beautiful, crisp winter evening in Jerusalem. Big bright stars were hanging low above the Judean hills and above the miniature model of Jerusalem in back of the Holyland Hotel. I was sitting with my daughter Smadar in the hotel's dining room waiting for our dinner guest. Punctually at 7:30, the time we had set, he arrived, a distinguished personality from Germany. After a fascinating conversation, in which we discussed art, theater, and literature, the inevitable came up: World War II. "You were probably not yet born during the war," he said. "I just managed not missing the event of the century," I told him. "You must have been just a baby—do you have any recollections?" "I do."

Yet somehow I did not want to speak about the Holocaust that night in Jerusalem, although our entire meeting had been arranged to discuss precisely that. "Did you ever witness an actual killing?" he continued to question me, almost interrogating me. "Yes, I did, one particular day...."

Before my eyes stood pictures of a small Lithuanian town, an empty street strewn with Jewish bodies dressed in their Sabbath finery. "Did you see Germans kill on that particular day?" "Only Lithuanian collaborators." "And Germans?" he continued to question me. "Yes, there was one German, but he did not shoot." I stopped short. Again, pictures kept flashing before my eyes, like slides projected on a screen: a small Jewish child dressed in a powder-blue velvet dress with a white lace collar crying for her mother; a Polish friend wrapped in a big shawl holding her by the hand; Grandma's house; a smiling German sitting in a window blowing the little girl a kiss while talking on the telephone. The big Polish woman picks up the little girl and covers her with a large woolen shawl. All is dark. The Polish woman whispers to her: "He is probably calling to report that all the Jews in Eisysky are dead. But we fooled him, my little one, you are alive."

"And what did you do during the war?" I asked him. He smiled, a good-natured smile. "Nothing exciting. I served in the Wehrmacht. I was a telephone operator...."

Yes. We were sitting in a hotel in Jerusalem. He told me that I could not have been in Europe during the Holocaust because I am too young. And after thanking him for the compliment, I told him that I was indeed in Europe during the Holocaust.

The only German I remember during the massacre in our little town in September, 1941 was a German telephone operator. He was sitting there, recording the numbers of the massacre. I saw him sitting in the window, and he waved at me, as a matter of fact, and smiled as he was reporting to his superiors the events in the town.

The German sitting across the table, a very prominent individual, told me, oh well, I didn't do much during World War Two, I was simply a telephone operator.

I had no sense of anger or hatred, just a sense of despair, a sense of trying to reach out, trying to overcome. He must have been no older than nineteen or twenty at the time. It became a symbol to me of the fact that every time a Jew and a German sit across the table, even with the best intentions, even in Jerusalem, their relationship is marred. I wanted to leave that sense of despair in the story. I did not want to end it on a hopeful note. This was, as I say, the non-Hasidic element in me, which I suspect was stronger, because it was my own tale rather than someone else's.

*For a moment, try to weigh those forms that you think have the greatest relevance in conveying the Holocaust theme. How would you measure documentary against fiction, against film?*

I really don't think they can be measured one against the other from an artistic point of view. Maybe as educational tools they can be measured. For the historian, it is obviously the documentary that ranks as the most important. And yet, for educational purposes, I do feel that, at times, it is the non-documentary film that has the greater impact on the individual or on our society. The documentary is for the few who are genuinely interested in the Holocaust and can bear being bombarded almost constantly with the terrible images of death and destruction of the Holocaust. Artistic films based upon fiction or novels may have a larger impact. I know there was quite a lot of opposition among people who teach the Holocaust to the *Holocaust* series. I felt that it was a way of reaching out to a much larger audience. I did not think the Holocaust was trivialized. I feel, however, that those who produce films have a greater responsibility to be more accurate when it comes to portraying events, but there are enough people who have that ability. So it's not a matter of ranking; it depends on the purpose.

*As long as there is fidelity to historical truth, the artistic approximations are acceptable to you?*

Yes, very much so. At the same time, our generation must stand guard that the events will not be distorted. This is, to me, the hallmark of everything that is being done and will be done with the Holocaust.

# George Steiner

George Steiner is one of the remarkable intellects of our time. Born in Paris in 1929, he moved to the United States, where he was educated at the University of Chicago and Harvard. He was awarded a Rhodes Scholarship and completed his doctorate at Oxford. He is presently Professor of English and Comparative Literature at the University of Geneva and Extraordinary Fellow of Churchill College, Cambridge.

Apart from his remarkable academic career, Steiner has written award-winning short stories, is an outstanding speaker, has worked for the *Economist* and as chief literary critic of *The New Yorker* magazine. His eclectic and wide-ranging insights are contained in such writings as: *The Death of Tragedy*, *After Babel: Aspects of Language and Translation*, *Nostalgia For the Absolute*, *Tolstoy or Dostoevsky*, *Anno Domini*, and *Language and Silence: Essays on Language, Literature and the Inhuman.*

George Steiner is, quite simply, awesome. I would ask a question, the hand-held microphone would hover at his lips, and Steiner, eyes fixed on some spot in the nether-distance, would launch into a spirited rhetorical torrent, words, ideas and analogies cascading brilliantly one upon the other until the point was made.

It was more a performance than an interview; but as can be seen, encyclopaedic in its scope.

---

*Recently there has been a spate of books and films in which the Holocaust theme has been central. Why now?*

The tragic and grim politics of Israel have thrown into extremely sharp relief the relationship between the Middle East crisis and the Holocaust, from which the modern state of Israel sprang. Anyone trying to think about the situation in the Middle East, which may bring on a world conflict, is almost bound to think about the Jewish flight to what was then Palestine, the emergence of the State of Israel, and the appalling paradox that, today, the Israeli Jew is in many respects the armed master of an occupied population. That's one reason.

Secondly, after an almost predictable interval, the figure of Hitler and the phenomenon of Nazism are again casting an immense spell over the imagination. The young and the ones who did not live through that period ask, "How was that possible? What kind of insane bad luck gripped mankind at that point?" Those who did live through it are just beginning to be able to bear their own memories. Psychologists tell us that there is a critical period before which you simply cannot endure or recollect what you have experienced. After thirty or forty years, not only can you begin to, but perhaps you have to, in order to come to some kind of peace with yourself.

*When you look at the materials that have emerged, how do you feel about them individually?*

I want to distinguish among those who actually went through it. If such a man says to me, "I will never write about it," hats off. I respect that very, very deeply. The German philosopher Adorno said, "No poetry after Auschwitz." (In fact, a better translation is, "No poetry about Auschwitz.") Simply keep your mouth shut, the thing is unspeakable. I say, "Right and fair." One has no right to challenge any survivor who chooses this option. There are also those, like Elie Wiesel, who have gone through it, and who feel they must bear witness the rest of their lives. That, too, I have enormous respect for.

Then there are those of us who have not personally endured it, and who feel we must come to grips with it. We've got to be terribly careful, because this theme flatters those who deal with it in a very subtle and corrosive way. The moment you set down the word Auschwitz or the theme of the death camps, you immediately pre-empt a certain kind of respect or importance or concentrated attention; we have to be very, very careful. There are great masters like Bill Styron—whom I admire—who, after writing as a black in *Nat Turner*, puts himself within the unimaginable skin of the Jews inside the death camps in *Sophie's Choice*, I think for profoundly honest and compelling reasons.

One must always ask what is the motive of the person who now takes up the Holocaust as a fiction, or a film, or a play, or an imaginary reportage. A book such as D.M. Thomas's *The White Hotel*, a world best-seller, has made many of its readers feel acutely uncomfortable, profoundly ill-at-ease when asking, "What is the motive behind this act of re-imagining?" So I don't think a general answer is possible to your question.

*In the past you have counselled self-restraint for those who deal with these themes. Here's Thomas moving from one*

*Holocaust in* The White Hotel *to another Holocaust in his recent book* Ararat, *with almost gratuitous ease. Does it disconcert you?*

Yes, deeply. I'm sure we're dealing with a serious writer—there's no question of it—and I don't mean this in any way to be *ad hominem*, but we've got to ask, what is the cost, even to the author, of writing a certain work. I think we have a right to ask what deposit he has put in the bank of terror and in the bank of transcendent mystery in order to make the big withdrawal of saying, "I was there in imagination."

We have so little powerful, active imagination in current literature, for all sorts of complicated reasons. We seem to be in a period of great criticism, great anthropology, great historical writing, very fascinating political writing. Yet the literary imagination, certainly, has been rather small beer after the time of Joyce, of Proust, of Kafka, of Mann, of Faulkner, to name the obvious ones. As we don't have the luxury of a Solzhenitsyn being in a kind of hell that compells our expression, perhaps a good many of us in the west subconsciously— not mendaciously, but not always carefully enough—have said to ourselves, "Ah, there is the big one. There is the one we don't need to invent. There is the one where we do not need to test our own poetic powers. It's lying there to be grabbed."

*You have wondered whether some of these novels would not ultimately be pulp fiction. Was that not a concern about* Sophie's Choice?

I hope not, because I think there is, in Styron, a very serious artist. Moreover, something wonderful happens in that book. All the American episodes seem brilliantly successful: the scene on the beach at Coney Island, the scenes in New York in the publishing world, the mad, apocalyptic trip to the south, Sophie utterly breathtaking. Yet I am unconvinced by the German and Polish scenes.

But that is a compliment to Styron. Finally he can't fake it. Finally his own honesty of talent brought a certain measure of failure to his attempt to imagine the unimaginable. I would have been much more worried if he had, in a techni-colour effect of virtuosity, been able to pull off the illusion of authority on the actual world of death camps; but I don't think he does.

*But for the world at large, the evocation of Sophie and the death camps is the death camps.*

You raise a very difficult point. There was a lot to criticize in the *Holocaust* television series, of course. Yet I think, on balance, it did a lot of good for the untutored or for the person who had done very little to find out what had happened in our own time and place. That television series, *Sophie's Choice*, *The White Hotel* and other works are bringing the imagination up against the unendurable. And that is such a monstrously difficult thing to do that it's too easy for us to take a very lofty view and say it needs a Tolstoy or Dostoevsky. Of course it does, but God doesn't always provide such writers; they aren't always available. Finally, the risks taken here are more honest, and have a far greater dignity of danger, than the next six hundred novels about adultery on the campus.

*Appelfeld says not only that the survivor alone can write with authenticity and emotive force, but also that the theme must be dealt with obliquely, if at all. You cannot deal with it head on.*

To the survivor who says that, I have nothing to answer. Neither you nor I has the right to say he is wrong. Yet Shakespeare creates for us, forever, the Venice of the Renaissance, the Rome of Julius Caesar, neither of which he had ever seen, and about which he knew less than does a modern school child. The fact that the great Napoleonic Wars against Russia exist for us in Tolstoy and not in the documents of the actual participants disproves Appelfeld's assertion. Again and again the great poet gets it right in a way that even the witness and the historian don't. I'd be very surprised if Homer had ever been within five hundred miles of Troy. I can see him listening to the distant survivors and saying to himself very gently, "I know better." And, in fact, he did. So I don't accept that.

But the question of obliqueness is a very real one. To do the oblique thing, to find the great metaphor that encloses a whole event, a period, a whole piece of history in an indirect and yet concrete way to make us feel it—God knows, that is rare. If you are Kafka, you can write a story about a man becoming a bug, and it can be shown that you have dreamed, in advance, the world of Auschwitz. There has been one Kafka. For the ordinary run of us, probably, trying to say certain things head on, though doomed to failure and often to embarrassment, is better than saying nothing at all.

*Is it likely that the Jewish spirit will fasten more and more on Kafka as time passes?*

There are now some hundred languages, including Mongolian and Japanese, in which the word "kafkaesque," meaning "like the world of Kafka," is spelled without a capital letter. A hundred languages in which, if you sit in an airport lounge or in a visa office or in a bureaucracy, or are in terror of faceless authority, the experience would be "kafkaesque," even to those who've never read Kafka, and may not even know that the word derives from a man's name.

This year we're celebrating the hundredth anniversary of his birth. At least two texts, *The Metamorphosis* and, even more, *In The Penal Colony* spell out, in almost exact detail, thirty years before the event, the world of the death camps. Kafka raises crucially the ancient and very beautiful enigma of the poet as prophet, the great writer as clairvoyant, a person uniquely gifted with anticipatory images. The late W.H.

Auden said, "If you have to name modern man, that figure which can be compared to Dante for mediaeval man, to Shakespeare for Renaissance man, it will be Kafka." And I think this is now universally true. But just remember that Kafka's four sisters, all four of them, and his beloved Milana, the central presence in his emotional life, perished in the very camps he dreamed in advance.

*How do you feel about the emerging preoccupation with the Holocaust theme in Germany itself?*

When we speak of current younger German writers, we're speaking of men and women who were not even born at the time, and I don't think we have any reason to put them in a category of predestined guilt. They are exactly as young as the rest of us, and to them, too, it is history in which they were not personally involved. The Germans are trying to do two things. There is an extremely honest attempt to come to grips with what happened in their own history. How did it happen? Why were my parents involved? An example is a very brilliant novella by Alfred Andersch about Himmler's father, who was a cruel but excellent teacher of ancient Greek in a small-town school. Andersch tries to read from a figure like that the coming monstrousness of absolute discipline and obedience. A very interesting oblique allegory.

Others are asking, "What is the rest of humanity like? What are the camps of the Soviet Union like? What is napalm like in Vietnam? What are the death squads of San Salvador doing? How does our experience relate to the more general problem?" Surely, when a German asks that, we have every reason to help him ask and to listen carefully to his answer.

*Do you feel that literature transcends film in conveying that theme?*

Yes. I belong to the very old-fashioned school. Even the greatest film can be seen only five times, six times, let's say seven times, and then it goes as dead as cold mutton, whereas you can re-read a text *ad infinitum* your whole life, and it will change with you, and you will change in your act of reading it. A film, of course, can carry to a mass audience an element of shock, of graphic information, of momentary images, perhaps stronger than the written word; but it is curiously short-lived and ephemeral. It is in the book that the transmission of the last shock can be achieved.

*Do you sense that films are more exploitive than books?*

I wouldn't want to generalize. There have been terrifying documentaries. One of the earliest, now forgotten, is Alain Resnais' *Night and Fog.* There have been some marvellous Italian evocations of the unimaginably bestial world of the Nazi rule of Rome and the north during the last months of the war in Europe. I understand that there is some very important Russian film material, which is not accessible to us. When you have the packaged, cellophaned horrors now beginning to prove so attractive on the big screen, surely the danger of exploitation is there; but it is also there in theatre, and in the novel. Exploitation is a general danger.

*You once wrote, with great feeling, about silence as a response to the Holocaust. One senses that your views are changing, or that sufficient time has passed to allow one to respond in a way that diminishes silence.*

I think your point is entirely fair. At that time, having read whatever was available, I felt that it was not adding to understanding. But a number of important things have happened since then: the French policy in Algeria, the long period of torture and massacre; the detailed revelations of the world of the Gulag, about which we knew generally, but certainly not in such massive and graphic detail; Vietnam and the great massacres in the Third World. All around us, the old and terrifying hunch that Hitler is part of a general phenomenon of twentieth-century politics and terror has become more and more pressing. I think this makes it imperative to grapple as best one can with the massacre of the Jews in Germany and its conquered territories in World War Two.

What is surprising, in some ways scary, and in some ways very moving, is the passionate interest of the young and their demand to know more. Wherever I go, wherever I lecture or give readings from my own work, it is the young who, either angrily or in sadness, either knowingly or in baffled ignorance, demand that this thing be discussed, that it be spoken of. I don't think we could have predicted that, and I'm not sure I know why it is happening. But almost anyone concerned with this field will confirm the phenomenon to you.

*Did the phenomenon assist in your decision to write your own novel,* The Portage To San Cristóbal Of A.H.*?*

That little novel "wrote" me; that is the only way I can put it. As I remember—and I remember rather vaguely the few weeks of its actual composition—I was not wholly in charge of the thing. I put it away for many years, not wanting to show it to anyone or to publish it. When the atmosphere changed it seemed necessary to take a chance and to see it into print.

Am I clear about my own motives? Was this a subtle form of self-flattery—perhaps not subtle at all—a gross form of psychological self-reassurance or self-flattery? Am I quite certain that, after a lifetime of critical writing, of theoretical writing, I didn't want to have a crack at the poetic imaginative form, because of my old hunch that somewhere a critic should give others a chance to go at him, that he should see if he can manufacture a pair of shoes after a lifetime of telling the rest of the world how to wear them? I'm not sure. The tangle of motives lies deep in the subconscious. Now the thing has mushroomed; it is getting out of my control. It is going into many languages; the dramatic versions are opening in several countries. Now the thing has its own life and its own imperative will.

*This is perhaps presumptuous: I was not so annihilated by the
finale, in which Hitler speaks; but I was stopped dead in my
tracks by Lieber's recitation of the death camps.*

Tell me that you remember. The garden in Salonika, where
Mordechai Zathsmar, the cantor's youngest child, ate excre-
ment; the Hoofstraat in Arnhem where they took Leah
Burstein and made her watch while her father; the two lime
trees where the road to Montrouge turns south, 8th November
1942, on which they hung the meathooks; the pantry on the
third floor, Nowy Swiat xi, where Jakov Kaplan, author of the
*History of Algebraic Thought in Eastern Europe 1280–1655,*
had to dance over the body of; in White Springs, Ohio, Rahel
Nadelmann who wakes each night, sweat in her mouth because
thirty-one years earlier in the Mauerallee in Hanover three
louts drifting home from an SS recruitment spree had tied her
legs and with a truncheon; the latrine in the police station in
Wörgel which Doktor Ruth Levin and her niece had to clean
with their hair; the fire raid on Engstaad and the Jakobsons
made to kneel outside the shelter until the incendiaries;
Sternowitz caught in the woods near Sibor talking to Ludmilla,
an Aryan woman, and filled with water and a piano wire wound
tight around his; Branka seeing them burn the dolls near the
ramp and when she sought to hide hers being taken to the fire
and; Elias Kornfeld, Sarah Ellbogen, Robert Heimann in front
of the biology class, Neuwald Gymnasium lower Saxony,
stripped to the waist, mouths wide open so that Professor Horst
Küntzer could demonstrate to his pupils the obvious racial, an
hour of school which Heimann remembered when at
Matthausen naked again; Lilian Gourevitch given two work
passes, yellow-colored, serial numbers BJ7732781 and 2, for
her three children in Tver Street and ordered to choose which of
the children was to go on the next transport; the marsh six
kilometers from Noverra where the dogs found Aldo Mattei
and his family in hiding, only a week before the Waffen-SS
retreated northward, thus completing the register of fugitives;
five Jews, one Gypsy, one hydrocephalic, drawn up at the
*prefettura* in Rovigo; the last Purim in Vilna and the man who
played Haman cutting his throat, remember him, Moritz the
caretaker whose beard they had torn out almost hair by hair,

pasting on a false beard and after the play taking the razor in the boiler room; Dorfmann, George Benjamin Dorfmann, collector of prints of the late seventeenth century, doctor and player on the viola, lying, no kneeling, no squatting in the punishment cell at Buchenwald, six feet by four and one-half, the concrete cracked with ice, watching the pus break from his torn nails and whispering the catalogue numbers of the Hobbemas in the Albertina, so far as he could remember them in the raw pain of his shaven skull, until the guard took a whip; Ann Casanova, 21 rue du Chapon, Liège, called to the door, asking the two men to wait outside so that her mother would not know and the old woman falling on to the bonnet of the starting car, from the fourth-floor window, her dentures scattered in the road; Hannah, the silken-haired bitch dying of hunger in the locked apartment after the Küllmans had been taken, sinking her teeth into the master's house shoes, custom-made to the measure of his handsome foot by Samuel Rossbach, Hagadio, who in the shoe factory at Treblinka was caught splitting leather, sabotage, and made to crawl alive into the quicklime while at the edge Reuben Cohen, aged eleven, had to proclaim "so shall all saboteurs and subverters of the united front," Hagadio, Hagadio, until the neighbors, Ebert and Ilse Schmidt, today Ebert Schmidt City Engineer, broke down the door, found the dog almost dead, dropped it in the garbage pit and rifled Küllman's closets, his wife's dressing table, the children's attic with its rocking horse, jack-in-the-box and chemistry set, while on the railway siding near Dornbach, Hagadio, the child, thrown from the train by its parents, with money sewn to its jacket and a note begging for water and help was found by two men coming home from seeding and laid on the tracks, a hundred yards from the north switch, gagged, feet tied, till the next train, which it heard a long way off in the still of the summer evening, the two men watching and eating and then voiding their bowels, Hagadio, the Küllmans knowing that the smell of gas was the smell of gas but thinking the child safe, which, as the thundering air blew nearer spoke into its gag, twice, the name of the silken-haired bitch Hannah, and then could not close its eyes against the rushing shadow; at Maidanek ten thousand a day; I am not mad, Ajalon calling, can you hear me; unimaginable because innumerable: in one corner of Treblinka seven hundred thousand bodies, I will count them now, Aaron, Aaronowitch, Aaronson, Abilech, Abraham, I will count seven hundred thousand names and you must listen, and watch Asher, I do not know him as well as I do you, Simeon, and Elie Barach and the boy, I will say Kaddish to the end of time and when time ceases shall not have reached the millionth name; at Belzec three hundred thousand, Friedberg, Friedman, Friedmann, Friedstein, the names gone in fire and gas, ash in the wind at Chelmno, the long black wind at Chelmno, Israel Meyer, Ida Meyer, the four children in the pit at Sobivor; four hundred and eleven thousand three hundred and eighty-one in section three at Belsen, the one being Salomon Rheinfeld who left on his desk in Mainz the uncorrected proofs of the grammar of Hittite which Egon Schleicher, his assistant newly promoted Ordinarius, claimed for his own but cannot complete, the one being Belin the tanner whose face they sprinkled with acid from the vat and who was dragged through the streets of Kershon behind a dung cart but sang, the one being Georges Walter who when they called him from supper in the rue Marot, from the *blanquette de veau* finely seasoned, could not understand and spoke to his family of an administrative error and refused to pack more than one shirt and asked still why why through his smashed teeth when the shower doors closed and the whisper started in the ceiling, the one being David Pollachek whose fingers they broke in the quarry at Leutach when they heard that he had been first violin and who in the loud burning of each blow could think only of the elder bush in his yard at Slanič, each leaf of which he had tried to touch once more on the last evening in his house after the summons came, the one not being Nathaniel Steiner who was taken to America in time but goes maimed nevertheless for not having been at the roll call, the one being all because unnumbered hence unrememberable, because buried alive at Grodne, because hung by the feet at Bialistok like Nathansohn, nine hours fourteen minutes under the whip (timed by *Wachtmeister* Ottmar Prantl now hotelier in Steyerbrück), the blood, Prantl, reporting, splashing out of his hair and mouth like new wine; two million at, unspeakable because beyond imagining, two million suffocated at, outside Cracow of the gracious towers, the signpost on the airport road pointing to it still, Oszwiecin in sight of the low hills, because we can imagine the cry of one, the hunger of two, the burning of ten, but past a hundred there is no clear imagining, he understood that, take a million and belief will not follow nor the mind contain, and if each and every one of us, Ajalon calling, were to rise before morning and speak out ten names that day, ten from the ninety-six thousand graven on the wall in Prague, ten from the thirty-one thousand in the crypt at Rome, ten from those at Matthausen Drancy Birkenau Buchenwald Theresienstadt or Babi-Yar, ten out of six million, we should never finish the task, not if we spoke the night through, not till the close of time, nor bring back a single breath, not that of Isaac Löwy, Berlin, Isaac Löwy, Danzig (with the birthmark on his left shoulder), Isaac Löwy, Zagreb, Isaac Löwy, Vilna, the baker who cried of yeast when the door closed, Isaac Löwy, Toulouse, almost safe, the visa almost granted, I am not mad but the Kaddish which is like a shadow of lilac after the dust of the day is withered now, empty of remembrance, he has made ash of prayer, AND UNTIL EACH NAME is recalled and spoken again, EACH, the names of the nameless in the orphans' house at Szeged, the name of the mute in the sewer at Katowic, the names of the unborn in the women ripped at Matthausen, the name of the girl with the yellow star seen hammering on the door of the shelter at Hamburg and of whom there is no record but a brown shadow burnt into the pavement, until each name is remembered and spoken to the LAST SYLLABLE, man will have no peace on earth, do you hear me Simeon, no place, no liberation from hatred, not until every name, for when spoken each after the other, with not a single letter omitted, do you hear me, the syllables will make up the hidden name of GOD.

*He* did it.

The man next to you now. Whose thirst and sour breath are exactly like yours.

Oh they helped. Nearly all of them. Who would not give visas and put barbed wire on their borders. Who threw stones through the window and spat. Who when six hundred escaped from Treblinka hunted down and killed all but thirty-nine— Polish farmers, irregulars, partisans, charcoal burners in the forest—saying Jews belong in Treblinka. He could not have done it alone. I know that. Not without the helpers and the indifferent, not without the hooligans who laughed and the soft men who took over the shops and moved into the houses. Not without those who said in Belgravia and Marly, in Stresa and in Shaker Heights that the news was exaggerated, that the Jews were whining again and peddling horrors. Not without D. initialing a memo to B-W. at Printing House Square: *no more atrocity stories. Probably overplayed.* Or Foggy Bottom offering seventy-five visas above the quota when one hundred thousand children could have been saved. Not alone.

But it was he who made real the old dream of murder. Everyman's itch to clear his throat of us. Because we have lasted too long. Because we foisted Christ on them. Because we smell other.

It was he who turned the dream into day. Read what he said to his familiars, what he spoke in his dancing hours. He never alludes to the barracks or the gas, to the lime pits or the whipping blocks. Never. As if the will to murder and the knowledge were so deep inside him, so much the core of his being that he had no more need to point to them. Our ruin was the air he moved in. We do not stop to count our breaths.

It was he. With his scourge of speech and divining rod. His wrist breaking each time he passed over other men's weakness. With his nose for the bestial and the boredom in men's bones. His words made the venom spill. Over to you, Simeon. Can you hear me?

Do you remember the photograph in the archive in Humboldtstrasse? Munich, August 1914, the crowd listening to the declaration of war. The faces surging around the plinth. Among them, partially obscured by a waving arm, but, unmistakable, his. The eyes upturned, shining. Within twenty-four months nearly every man in the photograph was dead. Had a shell found him out, a bullet, a grenade splinter, one of millions, the night would not have stood still over us. We would have grown old in our houses, there would be children to know our graves.

I'm extremely grateful to you, because for me Lieber's speech is the centre of the book. The scandalous feature, if you want, is Hitler's defence and our seeming inability to answer it. In the dramatic version, by the very gifted English political playwright Christopher Hampton, this became overwhelming, because Alex MacCowan is an actor of genius. He has just received the actor-of-the-year award for the part, and they showed that last speech on BBC television again. It was, indeed, unendurably triumphant, because it was spoken by a giant, who spellbound with every syllable everyone around him. The Lieber speech was also spoken by a very fine actor, but it is much more difficult to do in some ways.

Now, what is really fascinating and flattering—although one should not be flattered—is when reality begins catching up with fiction. The French press has just run a number of articles asking what would happen if the lawyers who are to be appointed to defend Klaus Barbi (the mass murderer recently brought back from South America to be tried in France) used Steiner's novel. They have been constructing defences for Barbi along the lines of my novel. This is terrifying and, at the same time, gives one a formidable sense of what fiction can do, in a way that perhaps criticism and philosophical argument are unable to do.

If I were Mr. Barbi, my defence would be extremely simple. I would get up and say, "Is there anybody on this bench, oh honourable judges, who decided not to be a judge, or decided to emigrate from France and join the resistance when the tortures were going on day and night in Algeria in the name of the French republic? If there is such a man, I accept him as my judge. If none of you is such a man, I have nothing more to say." And I would sit down.

*It reminds me of your observations in "Language and Silence" about timing and distance. Styron uses these as well: while the horrors were going on, the rest of us were eating and sleeping and making love and doing all the things that people normally do. Is it possible to bridge this moment of suspended irrationality? I don't know whether that would ever be resolved in fiction.*

Styron does me a great honour, as you know, in *Sophie's Choice*, to name me when he speaks of this. It comes at the beginning of one of Stingo's meditations; he has been reading my essay and speaks of this. I know no answer to this, but I don't want to shift it into the past. You and I are sitting in safety, in comfort, in friendship, in Toronto. At this very second, we know what is going on in the Russian psychiatric hospitals and in the torture chambers of Lubianka. You and I could say, perhaps, "Look, there is nothing on God's earth we can do about it." All right, it's not a comfortable answer; it's the first circle of hell.

Let's get a little closer to home. At this very minute, there are things going on in Nicaragua, Honduras, San Salvador and Costa Rica that are so unspeakable we couldn't talk about them on radio. It is said that in many parts of Assam, children are being buried alive or tortured to death. The comfortable answer, "I can do nothing about it," is beginning to wear thin. These events are not only much nearer, they are allegedly going on in the name of representative governments. These countries are the client states of America or Canada or the United Kingdom, to whom you and I pay our taxes, and which are meant to represent you and me in the corporate body politic.

So what will happen at the last judgement? What if the question is, "Never mind about the Gulag or Auschwitz, you were not there or you were not born or you could do nothing about it. But what did you do about those things that you *might* have been able to do something about, when you were sitting together, talking comfortably in a Toronto hotel room?" We are active accomplices of anything that leaves us indifferent.

*In "Language and Silence" you say that language has become bestial. Has it recovered from that bestiality?*

It has, I think, fallen into a gentler and larger bestiality. During the screening of *Holocaust* on American television networks, ads interrupted every fourteen and a half minutes. In the gas-oven sequences there were ads for panty-hose and detergents. I'm not sure a language or civilization can recover from that kind of thing. I'm literally not sure. "Recover" may be the wrong word. The civilization simply decides to accept a much lower level of human responsibility and human truth and human involvement. I would say that (and surely we will all be celebrating *ad nauseum* next year in 1984) Orwell's insight was to see that while one may get out from under the hell of Hitlerism and Stalinism, we may never be able to get out from under the mass-consumer society and the degeneracy of statements, and of the death of a certain level of verbal honesty.

*But you have pointed out a thousand times that people who read Goethe and listened to Beethoven went out and managed the death camps the next day. You asked yourself whether it is possible to re-establish a civilized humanness, whether it's possible to revive, through novels and film, a sense of human decency.*

You have me against the wall. If, as I'm convinced, a reading of Goethe or Shakespeare or Plato is no guarantee against being a butcher, it now looks as if mass-consumer-supermarket-bingo societies are no guarantee either. When I was much younger I asked, "Why is high culture no protection against bestiality?" It now looks as if that was a naïve question. Because it seems you can also be the average person—the most unideological, the most tolerant, the most relaxed, the most casual—and very little training can turn you into somebody who can burn people alive in Vietnam huts or bury them alive in San Salvador. So perhaps I come back to a more elitist, a sadder, a more classical position that says, if we have no choice, then I would like, perhaps very selfishly, to be of those who nevertheless read Goethe and Shakespeare and Plato, and who are not prepared to pull down theatres in order to build bingo halls.

*Let me speak with you of the distinctly Jewish response, if I may. Appelfeld is particularly unhappy about the assimilated Jew and the nature of German and Austrian society in the pre-war period. He has equal scepticism about the post-war assimilated Jew, even—dare I say it?—a little scepticism about George Steiner on those grounds. Is it possible to write with authenticity about the Holocaust theme, given the ambivalence you have about Israel and about your own Jewish associations?*

On the contrary, not only is it possible, it is essential, because Israel until very recently did not wish to touch the theme. Israel has taken that most mysterious saying of Jesus Christ, that great rabbi, "Let the dead bury the dead," and made it almost state policy. Israel is the one place where one was not to discuss the Holocaust. Why? Because Israel felt that there was, at the heart of the Holocaust, a terrible failure of Jewish courage, of Jewish resistance, of Jewish organization, of Jewish self-respect, and that this must never, never happen again. The Israel of Massada, and the Entebbe raid, and the Six Day War, is the one place on earth where the Jew does not need to evoke the horror of his long victimization.

In view of that, it is in the Diaspora, in the Jewish world outside Israel, that the Holocaust has to be continually remembered and dealt with. For if we Jews will not deal with Hitler, then no one will. The Germans do not want to deal with him much longer, so who will remember him? The whole allegory of my novel is that, if there is a *kaddish* to be said for the mystery of Hitler, it has to be said by Jews. For in our history he must never be allowed to be forgotten.

In my case, obviously, the use of fiction—a volume of stories called *Anno Domini*, which is tangentially about the Holocaust, and this little novel—is a way of searching for ideas, a wider audience, a more concentrated, more stimulating, perhaps lyric form. In a small earlier book, *In Bluebeard's Castle*, many of the arguments of the novel are already sketched. Everyone must choose for himself which version of

Jewish destiny or sensibility is his.

The State of Israel has to survive by the sword, day in and day out, night in and night out. I absolutely and profoundly respect the person who says, "I am going to Israel, or my children are going." I have much less respect for the parlour Zionist who talks Zionism from Manhattan or London, or Oxford or Cambridge or Toronto.

The Israel of the prophets and of Jeremiah—my Israel— is that which says, "You Jews have one mission: to be scattered among all human beings on earth, to be each other's guests, as men are guests of the planet, and the guests of life." Trees have roots, which is splendid. Men have legs, which is infinitely more marvellous. Men can move: they walk from language to language, from land to land, from profession to profession. And this movement has long been our genius and stimulus.

Isaac Amsel smiled in the dark.

—Gideon,

He didn't have to hurry now.

—Where will you go? I mean afterward. After we hand him over.

—Afterward? I'll go look for Adolf Hitler.

Isaac tried to choose the right laugh.

—You don't think that's he? You think we've got the wrong man? Are you serious?

He wanted to take the lamp and swing it close to Gideon's face.

—I don't know whether that's Hitler. Have you smelled him? He smelled too much like a man. He's got diarrhea. The scourge of God shouldn't smell that way. The real Hitler is inside the mountain. You haven't ever seen the *Riesengebirge,* like the mouth of an old leopard, white-and-gray teeth curving into the sky. The cold breath of those mountains hits you miles away. Listen to the pool, Amsel, listen.

The muffled booming of the gong passed just below them and drummed away into the unechoing forest.

—It's much louder than that in the mountains. That's

hiding, in the mouth of the black winds with the Re\_\_\_\_d and his armored men. They were Jew-killers too. You can draw gold out of a Jew's bladder if you squeeze hard enough. I read that, carved on the wall in the prison tower at Schwarzberg. I don't think he'd let himself be caught and done to death, not by a few scarecrows wading through a swamp. When a grenade bursts the sharp bits scatter. This is one of his splinters. Perhaps there are many flying about. The thousand-year *Reich* has hardly begun, count for yourself. I know when Hitler will die. I know the day. When the last Jew is dead. Then he'll shout once more, one last bellow, so loud that the mountains will crack, and he'll smile and fall dead on the stone table. But not until then. To be a Jew is to keep Hitler alive.

They heard Elie Barach's steps scuffing the sand as he went to the shelter, still mantled in his shawl.

—Why do you listen to me? Go to sleep. Check the paraffin and go to sleep.

—I want to go with you. Afterward.

—Where?

—To Paris.

Isaac felt such lightness in himself, piercing through the weight of sleep and the churn of his bowels, that he fluttered his hands before the hurricane lamp, a moth beating against the glass.

—To Paris. Where I'll study to become a film director. Oh I know it takes a long time. You've got to know languages; they make you spend six months in the cutting room just watching. But I'll become a director and write my own scripts. Like Jean Renoir. He's the greatest. I've seen everything he's done. I've seen *The River* five times. You remember when the flute stops sounding and you know that the snake has come? I'm going to make a picture about us, how Lieber's men went into the jungle and found Hitler. *Journey into the Green Hell.* Wide screen. No one has learned how to use a wide screen yet, not really. Antonioni faked it. I think he's really a still photographer. No film sense. I'll show how the Chavas surround us and won't let us go until we leave a hostage. Or until one of us fights against their best warrior using a spear set with piranha teeth. Long panning shot of the fight and the circle of spectators. I think I'll cast you in the part of the fighter. You'll win, of course, but we'll have to show a great scar. At the end we'll be seen staggering out of the jungle, bearded, limping, almost delirious, and a great crowd will surge toward us. I'll use a zooming lens to show a sea of faces, ecstatic, unbelieving. We'll hand Hitler over to the waiting guards. Press helicopters overhead, painted bright yellow, cameras looking at my camera. But I'll never show Hitler's face, not full on.

# D.M. Thomas

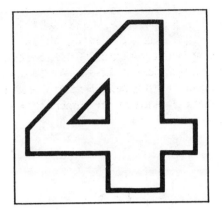

MARK GERSON

Novelist, poet and translator D.M. Thomas was born in Cornwall in 1935.

He has published seven collections of verse and is the recipient of a Cholmondeley Award for Poetry. His novels include *The Flute Player* which won the Gollancz Pan/Picador Fantasy Award, and *The White Hotel*, which won the 1981 Cheltenham Prize, the *Los Angeles Times* Fiction Prize and the P.E.N. Fiction Prize. His most recent novel is *Ararat*.

He has published four volumes of poetry translated from the Russian, works by Akhmatova, Pushkin and Yevtushenko.

D.M. Thomas lives in Hereford, England.

Thomas is the compleat articulate man. No question leaves him flustered or groping—even momentarily—for words. I had the sense that not only had he answered the same queries a thousand times, but that every prospective problem, contradiction or complexity was fully rationalized in advance.

With Thomas more than with anyone else, I walked away exhilarated, yet thinking anxiously of all the questions that should have been asked.

---

*You must have thought many a time in the last year or two about the remarkable reaction to* The White Hotel *and about the way in which it was embraced, in the United States in particular. Can you isolate what it is about the book that so engaged people?*

It's still very difficult to say. I suppose, for many readers, it created a breakthrough into what must have seemed to them rather forbidden sexual territory. Through that, they began to feel that they knew the heroine intimately; they identified with her fantasies and her preconceptions and her outlook on life. Therefore, when she met the Holocaust, it had a more personal effect on them than if they had read about it in another way, in an historical context. It is the association, the closeness of sex and death, of Eros and Thanatos—the great Freudian and great human forces—which, I think, either made people respond very strongly for it, or in some cases made them revolted by it.

*Did you have different reactions from Jewish and non-Jewish readers?*

Those Jewish readers who have contacted me have almost entirely been favourable in their response. They've felt sympathetic to my having tackled the theme. If I've received any criticism for tackling the Holocaust, it's nearly always been from non-Jews, particularly some middle-class English people, those with rather conventional ideas of what is acceptable in fiction. But I've been heartened by the fact that the Jews, on the whole, have been very responsive to it.

*Why do you think you chose the Holocaust as the ultimate expression of the life-and-death resolution?*

My own choice of it was in a way accidental. Of course, I have felt all my life, ever since I was about ten or eleven, when I saw the pictures from Belsen, that the Holocaust had changed life; that, whether you were Jewish or not, it added a new dimension to evil. The idea of mass anonymous death, the thought that so many people could be wiped out for no reason, in some ways threatened one's own sense of existence, one's own soul. I think life certainly has been different. Even now, forty years afterwards, there is a disturbance in the atmosphere because of what happened in the war, in places like Babi Yar and the concentration camps. But I never particularly wanted to deal with the Holocaust as a theme. I think it is very hard to encompass imaginatively, and I sympathize with all the people who feel that it's very dubious material. But I wanted to write a book in which my heroine would confront the forces of history in our times. As a central European, she would have to come up against them. Well, she wouldn't have to, but I wanted her to meet Freud, the humanism of Freud, and then, twenty years later, the inhumanity and the bestialism of Hitler. For me, there was really no choice: she had to meet the ultimate in evil, but the common fate of Jews in Europe. I didn't see any way of avoiding this.

Of course, the specific Babi Yar setting was touched off by reading the documentary material quoted in Kuznetsov's novel. I had certain moral choices to make then. But having decided, having got the idea for the novel and related it to some poems I had written two years before, and being very excited about the idea, I had no doubt that I should tackle this theme. However, I felt that the only way I could do it would be to not play around with the Holocaust, but to accept the physical descriptions of the eye-witness, of Dina Pronicheva, as reported by Kuznetsov. Everything else could be and should be imagination and fiction at play—and of course there is a certain fiction, in that Lisa has a child and she has her own life—but I wanted her to become merged in the actual historical reality. So I dealt with the Holocaust in fiction by, at the last moment, letting history take over.

They found themselves in a group that was being prodded to form a queue. Kolya asked if they were going to the train now, and she pulled herself together and told him, Yes, probably; and in any case she would be right behind him, and not to be afraid. Their group started to move forward. Everyone had fallen silent. They marched for some time in silence, between rows of Germans. Up in front could be seen more soldiers with dogs on leads.

Now they were in that long narrow corridor formed by two ranks of soldiers and dogs. The soldiers had their sleeves rolled up, and each of them brandished a rubber club or a big stick. Blows rained down, from both sides, on heads, backs, shoulders. Blood was running into her mouth but she hardly felt any of the blows, for she was trying somehow to protect Kolya's head. She felt the savage blows that landed on him—including the crunch of a club to his groin—but hardly at all those that landed on her own body. His scream was only one strand in a universal scream, mixed with the happy shouts of the soldiers and the barking of dogs, but it was the one that stood out, even above her own. He stumbled; she gripped his arms and kept him from falling. They were trampling straight over fallen bodies that had been set upon by the dogs. "Schnell, schnell!" laughed the soldiers.

They tumbled out into a space cordoned off by troops, a grassy square, scattered with articles of clothing. The Ukrainian police grabbed hold of people, hitting them and shouting: "Get your clothes off! Quickly! Schnell!" Kolya was doubled up with pain, and sobbing, but she started fumbling at his shirt collar. "Quickly, dear! Do as they say." For she saw that anyone who hesitated was being kicked, or struck with a knuckleduster or club. She pulled off her dress and her slip, then took off her shoes and stockings in between helping her son, because his hands were shaking and he couldn't deal with shirt buttons and shoe laces. A policeman started hitting her with his club, on her back and shoulders, and in her panic she couldn't unhook her corset fast enough, and the policeman, growing more and more angry with the slow-witted, flabby-breasted old woman, ripped the corset from her body.

There was a moment's peace, now that they were undressed. One group of naked people was being herded off somewhere. Fumbling among discarded clothes for her hand-bag, Lisa took a handkerchief from it and gently wiped some of the blood and tears from Kolya's face.

She saw her identity card in her bag, and came to a quick decision. Among the white shapes of dazed demented people she saw a German officer who looked as if he might be in charge. She walked determinedly up to him, thrust the identity card in his face and said in German that she and her son were there by mistake. They had come to see someone off, and become trapped in the crowd. "Look!" she said. "I'm a Ukrainian woman married to a German." The officer, frowning, muttered that too many mistakes of this kind were being made. "Put on your clothes and go and sit on that hillock." He pointed to where a handful of people were sitting. She rushed back and told Kolya to dress quickly and come with her.

Everyone on the hillock was silent, crazed with fright. Lisa found she could not take her eyes off the scene which was being enacted in front of them. One group of people after another came staggering out of the corridor, screaming, bleeding, each of them to be seized by a policeman, beaten again and stripped of clothes. The scene was repeated over and over again. Some were laughing hysterically. Some became old in minutes. When Lisa's gift or curse of second sight had failed her so miserably and her husband was snatched away in the dark, her hair had gone grey overnight—the old saying was true. But now she saw it happen in front of her eyes. In the next group but one after theirs she saw Sonia; and her raven hair turned grey in the time it took for her to be stripped and sent away to be shot. Lisa saw it happen again and again.

There was a steep wall of sand, behind which the firing could be heard. They made the people form up into short lines and led them through the gap which had been hurriedly dug in the sandstone wall. The wall hid everything from view, but of course the people knew where they were. The right bank of the Dnieper is cut by deep ravines, and this particular ravine was enormous, majestic, deep and wide like a mountain gorge. If you stood on one side of it and shouted you would scarcely be heard on the other. The sides were steep, even overhanging in places; at the bottom ran a little stream of clear water. Round about were cemeteries, woods and allotments. The local people knew the ravine as Babi Yar. Kolya and his friends had played in it often.

She saw that, as the men and women were led through the gap, they all without exception clasped their hands over their genitals. Most of the children did so too. Some of the men and boys were in agony from blows there, but it was mostly an instinctive shame, of the kind that made Kolya not want her to see him undressed. He too, on stripping, had put his hands there, partly because of pain, but also out of natural modesty. It was the way Jesus had been buried. The women were trying to cover their breasts too, with their arms. It was terrible and strange to see them concerned for their modesty, while they were being taken away to be shot.

Kolya still had his hands clasped between his thighs. He was hunched forward, and could not stop shivering. He could not stop, even though she hugged him and warmed him and tried to whisper comforting words. And he said nothing. Speech had been shocked out of him.

She knew she herself must keep from breaking down altogether, even when Liuba Shchadenko staggered out of the corridor, clasping hold of her youngest, Nadia. The mouth of the three-year-old was open wide in a soundless howl. Liuba's face was covered in blood, as were the faces of Olga and Pavel, who staggered out after her. There was no sign of old Mrs Shchadenko. For an instant, just after she had pulled her dress over her head, Liuba seemed to look straight at her friend on the hillock, accusingly. But she could have seen nothing at that moment. When she had stripped, she started fussing with the buttons of Nadia's frock, but too slowly. A policeman grabbed the child angrily, carried her like a sack of potatoes to the sandstone wall and flung her over.

"Hail Mary full of grace..." "Ora pro nobis..." Lisa mumbled the prayers of her childhood as the tears pressed out between her eyelids.

No one could have imagined the scene, because it was happening. In spite of the shouts, the screams, and the patter of machine guns, Lisa heard nothing. As in a silent film, with the white cumulus drifting across the blue sky. She even started to believe that nothing terrible was happening beyond the wall of sand. For nothing could be worse than this, or as bad. She did not know where the people were being taken, but they were not being killed. She said as much to Kolya. "We're just being frightened. You'll see, we'll go home and then Pavel and the others will turn up safe and sound." She had always found it difficult to kill even a cockroach; and there was simply no reason to kill all these people. The Germans were lining the people up, firing over their heads at the ravine side, laughing at the joke, and telling them to get dressed in fresh clothes and go and sit in the train. It was mad, but not so mad as the alternative. She went on half believing it even after she heard a Ukrainian officer say the words: "We'll shoot the Jews first and then let you out."

Those words were spoken to a young woman she had known slightly in the old days—Dina Pronicheva, an actress at the Kiev puppet theatre. Lisa recognized her as she staggered out of the corridor. Two old people, perhaps her parents, waved to Dina from another group, probably telling her to try to get away. Instead of taking off her clothes, Dina marched up to the Ukrainian officer who was standing in front of the hillock, and Lisa heard her demand to be let out. She showed him the contents of her bag. She certainly did not look Jewish—less so even than Lisa, with her rather long nose. Dina's surname was Russian and she spoke Ukrainian. The commander was convinced, and spoke the words about letting her out later. Dina now saw a few places away, lower down the hillock. Like most there, she kept her head buried in her arms: from shock, grief, and perhaps also from fear lest someone recognize her and shout, "She's a dirty Yid!", hoping to save their own skin.

Lisa remembered a prayer her nurse had taught her, to protect her from nightmares: "You who are Saviour..." There are things so far beyond belief that it ought to be possible to awake from them. But, although the prayer helped her a little, the nightmare continued. The world was a world of little children being hurled over a wall like sacks of grain being thrown on to a waggon; of white soft flesh being flailed as peasant women flailed drying clothes; the shiny black boot tapped by the black whip of the bored officer standing in front of the knoll. "You who are Saviour..."

She felt helpless to help Kolya. There was nothing to do but to pray selfishly that all the others might be killed, with merciful speed, and those on the hillock allowed to go home. She prayed this selfish prayer continuously. But she did not once regret she had not accepted Liuba's offer and stayed behind. Now she knew why she ought never to have had children. And yet the thought of Kolya, her son, being here with strangers, perhaps in that group of children from the orphanage, was a hundred times worse than the terror of death.

She passed into a trance, in which everything that was being enacted before her happened slowly and without sound. Perhaps she had literally become deaf. It was quieter than the quietest night. And the clouds drifted across the sky with the same terrible, icy, inhuman slowness. Also there were changes of colour. The scene became tinted with mauve. She watched cumulus gather on the horizon; saw it break into three, and with continuous changes of shape and colour the clouds started their journey across the sky. They were not aware of what was happening. They thought it was an ordinary day. They would have been astonished. The tiny spider running up the blade of grass thought it was a simple, ordinary blade of grass in a field.

The afternoon, that was no conceivable part of time, wore on, and it started to get dark.

Suddenly an open car drew up and in it was a tall, well-built, smartly turned-out officer with a riding crop in his hand. At his side was a Russian prisoner.

"Who are these?" the officer asked the policeman, through the interpreter, pointing to the hillock, where there were about

"They are ou... ...s. They were seeing people off; they ought to be ... ...

Lisa heard the officer shout: "Shoot the lot at once! If even one of them gets out of here and starts talking in the city, not a single Jew will turn up tomorrow."

She caught hold of Kolya's hand and gripped it tight, while the interpreter translated the officer's order, word for word. The boy started to pant for breath, and his hand shook violently but she tightened her grip. She whispered: "God will take care of us, darling—you'll see." A sudden sharp unpleasant smell told her he had lost control of his bowels. She hugged him tightly and kissed him; now the tears she had bottled up for most of the day rolled down her cheeks. He had neither cried nor spoken all the time they had been sitting on the knoll.

"Come on then! Let's go! Get yourselves up!" the policeman shouted. The people stood up as if they were drunk. They were quiet and well behaved, as if they were being told to go and have some supper. Maybe because it was already late the Germans did not bother to undress this group, but led them through the gap in their clothes.

Lisa and Kolya were among the last. They went through the gap and came out into a sand quarry with sides practically overhanging. It was already half dark, and she could not see the quarry properly. One after the other, they were hurried on to the left, along a very narrow ledge.

On their left was the side of the quarry, to the right a deep drop; the ledge had apparently been specially cut out for the purposes of the execution, and it was so narrow that as they went along it people instinctively leaned towards the wall of sandstone, so as not to fall in. Kolya sagged at the knees and would have fallen, but for his mother's grip on his arm.

They were halted, and turned to face the ravine. Lisa looked down and her head swam, she seemed so high up. Beneath her was a sea of bodies covered in blood. On the other side of the quarry she could just see the machine guns and a few soldiers. The German soldiers had lit a bonfire and it looked as though they were making coffee on it.

She gripped Kolya's hand and told him to close his eyes.

He would not feel any pain and when they were in heaven she would be with him still. She saw his eyes close. She thought of telling him that his daddy and his real mummy were already there to meet him; but decided it was the wrong thing to do. A German finished his coffee and strolled to a machine gun. She started to whisper the Lord's Prayer, and heard her son's faint voice beside her saying it too. She did not see as much as feel the bodies falling from the ledge and the stream of bullets coming closer to them. Just before it reached them she pulled Kolya's hand, crying "Jump!", and jumped with him off the ledge.

*There is obviously a feeling among many that the Holocaust must be dealt with only in authentic historical terms or in terms described by eye-witnesses, and that to attempt a fictional account is to risk trivializing or degrading the event. Are you saying that you bridged that apprehension by turning to the eye-witness account?*

Exactly. I got attacked in the press for doing so, but for me it was the only ethical way I could deal with the Holocaust. I agree with the people who say that you shouldn't fictionalize it. It's too real and still too painful for people who lost parents and so on. Simply, my imagination failed before it. So what I did was to bring my fictional heroine closer and closer to Dina Pronicheva, the actual survivor, and to make it clear in the text and also in acknowledgments that I was doing so. My heroine was in the same group, the last group of Babi Yar, and what Dina saw, my heroine saw. For a while, therefore, they move step by step with each other, and fiction becomes dissolved for a few moments in history. That was the only way I could deal with it. Lisa's *thoughts* are her own but what she *saw* could only be the historical reality.

*Why do you think that there is a pre-occupation with the Holocaust theme at this time?*

I haven't thought about it deeply, but I suspect that there

is more than one reason and that some are more worthy than others. I suspect there has, to some extent, been a kind of fashion created, and, God help me, I may have helped to create the fashion. Certainly when one writer deals with a theme, then others feel that it can be tackled also. And I suppose simply there is the distance in time; it is now a generation or more ago. We were for years numbed with horror. Then there was the setting up of the State of Israel, and the discovery that history has moved on and that even Israel itself can sin. Perhaps now it's time to reflect on what happened.

*Part of the reason your book is so riveting is surely the conjunction of sexuality and the Holocaust. Why the link? Was it purely Eros and Thanatos? Or was it more? In the minds of some readers, the sexual pathology and culmination in the Holocaust are not naturally related.*

I felt there were a number of links, which seemed entirely natural. Reading about Babi Yar reminded me of the poem I had written and therefore of Freud. I was reminded, first of all, of comparisons, of analogies: the victims were Jews; Freud's patients were almost entirely Jews; the analysts were almost entirely Jews. It was a kind of Jewish collective psychoanalysis originally, and a kind of alternative religion. And maybe it was a defence against anti-Semitism, in part. Those were the connections. Then there were also contrasts. It seemed to me that Freud's penetration into sexuality was liberating individuality. He was saying that each individual, though perhaps governed by certain general laws, was unique; every woman who came into his consulting room had a history like Clytemnestra or Electra. There was something heroic and noble in this battle, which went on in every individual's mind. And Freud would spend months and sometimes even years, day in and day out, trying to get deeper and deeper into a human soul. (And when he said *psyche*, he meant soul and not mind, as we very often interpret it.) In contrast, when Hitler came along, far from studying any individual soul, he wiped out thousands or millions with no thought. There was a sudden chasm between individualism, as it flourished with Freud, and the brutal wiping out of humanity. The scenes of the Holocaust were like something out of Bosch, or some nightmarish artist. They were far more fantastic and nightmarish than anything that a patient of Freud's had suffered from. Then it occurred to me that perhaps a Jew in that generation would have had some kind of intuition, some premonition of the future, and that the febrile, nervous state that Freud investigated might be, in part, a projection from the future, rather than from childhood, as he thought. It all seemed to link in together. Also, of course, some of the images of Babi Yar—burning the hair and the fall into the ravine—linked up, in an odd, coincidental way, with the images of violence that I had found quite instinctively in my poem. So, for me, it was an inevitable metaphor. But I can't persuade readers of that: it either seems to work or it doesn't, but that's how it came about.

Freud said that the sexual instinct is where the highest and the lowest are closest together. He quoted Goethe from "Heaven Across The World to Hell." I think the sexual instinct does embrace totality; I think it does embrace everything. You have extremes: St. Theresa feeling the arrows of God; a Jack the Ripper or necrophilia—again an unimaginable horror. And most of us, most ordinary human beings, like you or I, are seemingly in the middle, neither with the seraphic visions of St. Theresa or the loathsome fantasies of a Jack the Ripper. But nevertheless, in our own sexuality, at times we touch both extremes in a way, if only through fantasy. We touch apprehensions of the divine and at times we are aware of dark forces in us, a desire to be cruel, or sado-masochistic, if only as a kind of brief shadow. Whether this embraces the Holocaust, I don't know, but it certainly embraces death and violence; and as that is an extreme form of violence, there is a possibility that it might touch our imagination in that way, which I think is a horrific thought if it is true. I think it is thrown up by *The White Hotel* in some way, and maybe that is why some people become very agitated by it. But if it is human, perhaps it is better to confront that. Just because someone finds an erotic fantasy in something very dark doesn't mean that he or she is going out to do it. It is better, in that case, to confront it, as Freud was doing, to try to bring up these dark forces, to bring them into the light. I think the answer, which Freud quotes from Goethe, is "more light, more light."

*The anti-Semitism of which Babi Yar is the ultimate expression emerges hardly at all in the Freudian analysis of your heroine. I was struck by the fact that, aside from the letters at the outset, so much of the book goes by before the anti-Semitic aspect is dealt with. I wondered how an analyst of Freud's stature could have spent so much time with your heroine without plumbing that depth.*

That's an interesting question. Freud himself, in his genuine cases, didn't deal much with Jewishness. There was a part of him that evaded the problem of anti-Semitism. Certainly until as late as possible, he lingered on in Vienna and hoped for the best. There were times when he would react against anti-Semitism, but I can't remember a time in any of his cases, even though his patients were Jewish, where he deals with a racial matter. I think he was defensive about it to a great extent. Also, I have to admit, it seemed to fit the form of the novel that there shouldn't be too many sign-posts of the Jewishness.

Also Lisa was a very cunning woman, a very cunning patient. It was her way of fighting off Freud. I think that analysis is, in part, a sort of sexual battle, an attempted seduction on the analyst's part, and the patient's only defence is lies and evasion. At least that's how Lisa sees it. I admire her for lying to Freud. She had very bad experiences tied up with her Jewishness. When she was in Odessa as a child she met an anti-Semitic attack, as you may remember. At that time there were already pamphlets in Russia saying that the Jews should be wiped out. So she has every reason to suppress her Jewishness. And when Freud mentions being Jewish, she says to him, "Jewishness is nothing to me. I think of myself as a mid-European Christian." She had converted to Catholicism. She would have said that so lightly and naturally that Freud, given his already existing tendency to evade the subject, was quite willing not to pursue it. There were so many other clues from her past that I could see him being drawn inexorably down the wrong path and forgetting about the Jewishness altogether. I think it was justified.

*Lisa's second sense, her foreboding, the sense the reader has almost from the outset that there's something coming—these for you are absolutely central, aren't they?*

Yes, it was the whole meaning of the book, that events in the future could flow back to the present, which I think they do. I think there must be an awful lot of hysteria or nervous tension now as a result of our fears about a nuclear holocaust, for example. There is traditionally an association of powers of prediction with hysteria. Hysterical women like Sibyl at Delphi or like Cassandra at Troy were given powers of prophesy seemingly as a kind of compensation for their madness. The very word *hysteria* is tied up with the womb, which sends forth the child, and is perhaps afraid of what will happen to that child. I'm talking off the top of my head, but, yes, I think hysterical patients probably always have had an intuitive gift. So again, it seemed to me entirely natural that Lisa should have these powers of intuition.

*Why is it so often women? Why do novelists so often choose women as those who are sacrificed in this ultimate crucible? It can be said that the combination of the Holocaust with sexual innuendo has a certain pornographic quality. And it always seems to be focussed on the woman, as it is in* The White Hotel. *Why do you think that is?*

Well, I can only answer for myself. Most of Freud's patients were women, to start with, and the work had begun unconsciously with a woman speaking, so it was inevitable that it should be a woman. I think there are very good reasons women and not men had hysterias. I hinted at it by mentioning the womb, which is the original meaning of the word. Hysteria is an apprehension for the future, for the child. Women have more stake in the future. But I don't see it at all pornographically. Holocausts are made by men. You may have a few sadistic women camp guards, but there would never have been a Holocaust without males. For me, it is natural to have an innocent and vulnerable creature, a woman, being the victim of male Fascism. Lisa, in a way, embodies the good, life-giving virtues, which are crushed by male force. I would see it entirely differently from those who would say this is pornographic. It all depends whether anyone feels that there's some pornographic pleasure in having a woman bayoneted in Babi Yar, or gunned down. I don't think there is. I don't think it is pornographic in the least.

*So the mesh of sexual fantasy at the outset with the ultimate expression of horror in the finale is, for you, the resolution of those twin themes. And anybody who would interpret it otherwise simply does not understand what you were attempting to say.*

Yes, here is a woman whose sexuality is, in its essence, healthy. This fact comes out clearly in all the images of giving in *The White Hotel:* the milk that flows freely for all, the lack of selfishness. But she is constantly threatened by darker forces. The reason for those apprehensions becomes clear at the end, when maleness kills her and her child.

*Are you puzzled by the inclination to view the book as manipulative, to view it as imposing the Holocaust on a life that, organically, doesn't quite seem to lead there, except in your mind?*

What do you mean by "organically"?

*Well, once Lisa is off with Victor in Russia, the reader is not quite prepared for the leap into Babi Yar. It truly jolts. Everything else in the novel flows so organically from the early poetry, and the exposition, and the case book, and then suddenly the reader is plunged into Babi Yar. It is as though the Holocaust were a sudden insertion, a sudden imposition on the book. Some readers might feel that using the Holocaust that way is manipulative.*

Well, one person's manipulation is another person's art. The Holocaust must have come like that to people, with sudden and unexpected violence. Until the last minute they thought they were going to Israel, and then there was a horrifying moment when suddenly the whips were out and the dogs were barking and they were told to undress and go to their deaths. It was like that. Obviously, I had the choice of going through the year leading up to Babi Yar, which would have involved the terror and Victor being taken away. I could have dealt with the Stalinist terror. But for me, then, that would have been an irrelevance. I needed to concentrate on just one horror. I wasn't writing an epic family narrative of life in Soviet Russia, in which one would have had the knock in the night and Victor been taken off to prison and to Siberia. I decided that, artistically, it was best to take them to a point where life was hard but they were at least surviving. And then relate just one day when the Holocaust came. It was an artistic decision; it wasn't manipulative. I can understand why people who dislike the book could find it manipulative. They are seeing the hand of the controlling author at work. Those who do respond to it and are moved would see it as art. I can only say that, as it was written organically, and I know that I wasn't manipulating. And if I were to write it again, I'd still do it in that way.

*Talk for a moment about the final chapter.*

After the chaos and overcrowding of the nightmarish journey they spilled out on to the small, dusty platform in the middle of nowhere. They struggled over a little bridge; then it was good to breathe the sweet air, and to be ushered through without bullying or formalities. Outside, there was a line of buses waiting.

The young lieutenant in charge of Lisa's bus had a diffident stammer which relaxed the atmosphere as he read out the roll. He smiled shyly when the passengers' chuckles told him he had got one of the difficult names wrong. He had particular trouble with Lisa's. Under a film of sweat—the day was very hot—a white scar ran up his cheek and across his forehead, and a sleeve rested uselessly in his uniform pocket.

As the bus moved off in a cloud of dust, he swung himself into the empty seat in front of Lisa. "Sorry about that!" He smiled. "Don't worry!" She smiled back. "It's Polish, I take it?" he inquired; and she confirmed it was so. Actually, she was embarrassed by her error. Having decided not to use her Jewish name, Berenstein, nor her German name, Erdman—because of all the harassment she had been through when asked to produce her documents—she had wished to give her maiden name, Morozova. But for some strange reason she had given her mother's maiden name instead: Konopnicka. It was too late now to do anything about it. The young lieutenant was asking her how the train journey had been. "Terrible! Terrible!" said Lisa.

He nodded sympathetically, and added that at least they would be able to rest at the camp. It wasn't a palace, but it was fairly comfortable. Then later they would be sent on further. Lisa said he would never know how much it meant, to hear a friendly voice. She looked out at the monotonous desert, under the burning sky, and missed his next question, about what she did in her previous life. He had to repeat it. He was pleased to hear she was a singer. Though he didn't know much about music, he enjoyed it, and one of his tasks was to arrange concerts at the camp. Perhaps she would be willing to take part? Lisa said she would be glad to, if her voice should be thought good enough.

"I'm Richard Lyons," he said, offering her his left hand over the back of the seat. Awkwardly she shook it with her own wrong hand. The name stirred a memory; and astonishingly it turned out she had known his uncle. She had met him while on holiday in the Austrian Alps. "He thought you were dead," she said; and Lieutenant Lyons said, with a wry grin, "Not quite!" and patted his empty sleeve. Of course he knew the hotel where she had stayed, for he had skied there often.

"It's a beautiful place," he said.

"Yes, but so is this," she replied, glancing out again at the sand dunes. "It's a beautiful world."

She took the opportunity to ask him how one should set about trying to trace relatives. He took a notebook and a pencil from his breast pocket and, using his left hand adroitly, both to grip the notebook and to write in it, wrote the name Berenstein. He promised to make some inquiries. "You can be sure your relatives will be scanning the new lists too," he said. She thanked him for his kindness and he said it was nothing, he was happy to help.

*Why is it there?*

It was a late thought in the writing of the book. I had assumed originally that it would end at Babi Yar, but then I realized that although I had dealt with this human being sexually and cerebrally and intellectually in the Freudian analysis, and in terms of her vocation, I missed out the spiritual side of her. I decided there ought to be some kind of spiritual fantasy at the end, as there is a sexual fantasy, and as there is Freud's fantasy of who she is. It also increasingly became clear to me that it would falsify the book to end with the blackness of Babi Yar; that what I was saying in the book, or struggling to say, was that the light is a little stronger than the dark, that at the end of *The White Hotel* poems and fantasies, there is some feeling of goodness. When the hotel guests sign out, they say "back next year" or those kind of banal phrases you use in hotel guest lists. On the whole, one prefers to live rather than not to live, or I do. Therefore at the end of the book, there should be some re-assertion of this life principle.

It then became a matter of finding a metaphor. The clue was given to me by the suggestions that the Jews at Babi Yar did think they were going to be sent to Israel. I thought of the fact that Israel was being founded. It was a kind of rocky state, very much like Purgatory in Dante, painful but with a kind of purity and a purpose and a quest. So I decided to have Lisa dream that she was there, or to have her there. I wasn't clear whether this was an after-life vision, or simply another dimension to the book. I felt that the language should be somewhere between realism and mysticism, that it should have a dream-like quality and yet also a kind of dogged reality of bumping along in a bus to a camp. I thought the imagery of the Song of Songs would be appropriate, too, to give that sort of religious dimension to it, and that people should still be suffering, but that the suffering should have a meaning, as opposed to the unmeaning of Babi Yar, that the meaning would be its own redemption, its curing. And so we see Freud being healed and Lisa's mother still being healed and Lisa herself beginning to be healed. This was a kind of religious statement, a search or quest. I think the whole book is a quest. It is dominated largely by a train journey of one kind or another.

The last section has been misunderstood by lots of critics. Some, for example, have said it is a kind of paradise, which it certainly isn't. It's more like Dante's Purgatory. One or two have even said that it's a kind of promotion of Zionism, which was very far from my intent. It is a metaphor; it is not the real land of Israel, because there are also non-Jews there. It is perhaps, in the end, my quest for meaning. Perhaps it says that, faced with an experience like the Holocaust, there is no salvation within history, that if there is healing, it is somewhere beyond history.

# Jurek Becker

ALEXANDER BECK

Jurek Becker was born in Lodz, Poland in 1937. After the Nazi invasion of Poland, he was imprisoned in a concentration camp. After liberation he moved to Berlin, where he finished his schooling and studied philosophy.

Since 1960 he has been a freelance writer, creating film and cabaret scripts, television plays, and a volume of short stories, as well as five novels including *Jacob the Liar* and *Misleading the Authorities*. He is the recipient of many awards, among them the Heinrich Mann and Charles Veillon prizes, the City of Bremen literary prize, the National Prize of the German Democratic Republic and the coveted title of Resident Poet of Bergen-Enkheim (Frankfurt).

Becker now lives in West Berlin.

Jurek Becker is not an easy man to assess: there is an elusive quality about him, a certain sense of mystery. I was never quite sure whether the dynamic of the interview was disarming candour or impish manipulation. To be fair, however, Becker was most uncomfortable in English. This was his first-ever all-English interview (there was an interpreter hovering throughout), but as the reader will see, language proved no impediment whatsoever.

---

*How was it that you went to Germany after 1945?*

I was born in Poland in 1937. My family was in a concentration camp—my mother died there, and my father and I were the only survivors from our family. At the end of the war I was in Sachsenhausen and he was in Auschwitz. He found me with the help of an American organization. I was seven years old.

It was my father's decision to stay in Berlin. I often asked him why. He never gave me a clear explanation, but once he said, "When there is no place you feel good, then you can stay wherever you are." At the time he said, "I think a result of the war is the defeat of the German anti-Semite, not of the Polish anti-Semite." I think that's another reason he stayed in Germany.

A third reason was that all his roots in Poland had been cut off—all his family was dead. Yet in Berlin, after the war, he did know some people who had also been in the concentration camp. They were his only "relations." He never spoke about it, but I think an important reason was that when you come out of a camp, you are terribly tired—you are too tired to move. You just want to stay where you are.

*You spent most of your adult life in East Germany, in fact.*

Not most, *all* of it.

*Do you feel that the East German perspective on the war period is different from that of West Germany?*

I think so. First, the East German government sees itself not as the successor to a former Germany, but as if there were nothing before it began in 1945. They do not feel that the history of Germany is a history of East Germany. They try to teach the people that the Germanies are two different countries, two different entities. Once my son came home from school—he was six years old or so—and he asked, "Father, is it true that Hitler invaded East Germany?" It sounds like a joke, but I think it's indicative of what is happening in East Germany.

Moreover, after the war, when the border was still open, people moved between east and west. The Nazis feared the Russians more than they feared the Americans, or the English and French soldiers. And they were right to fear them more, because the Nazis had done more to the Russians. So they moved to the west. The anti-Fascists had greater hopes of the Russians. Never mind what actually happened—at the time they expected help from them. And that's why most of them moved to the east. So there are more former Fascists in the west and more anti-Fascists in the east.

A very important thing is that most of the members of the government in East Germany were members of the underground against the Nazis during the war, and this gives them a particular outlook on the problem of anti-Semitism. I am sometimes asked if I watch out for anti-Semitic actions or feelings in East Germany, but I always answer, "Never." It's not because there aren't any, but I think they are much more severely punished than in the west. So people who might like to say anti-Semitic things keep their mouths shut.

*Does this East German perspective give you a particular approach or view as an artist when speaking of the Holocaust period?*

I am sure that it does, but I don't know how it works. And I don't want to know. I'm not interested because I fear that if I think too much about it, it will upset everything. It's like a fable I once heard, by La Fontaine. A centipede was walking through a forest and a snail fell in love with him. "I admire you so much," said the snail. "How do you walk like that? You have so many legs and feet, and you never mix them up. It's wonderful to see you walk. How do you do that?" The centipede felt flattered and said, "Oh, I don't know, I never thought about it. Wait a minute, I'll think about it." And he started to think and couldn't walk any more. That's the problem.

*One of your most charming characteristics is that you frequently deny the things that are said of you. Melvin Kornfeld, who translated your book,* Jacob the Liar, *into English, sees it as part of Holocaust literature. Yet at a recent panel discussion you strongly disavowed that. You were bothered by it. Why?*

What he says is his business, and what I say is my business—we are not members of one political party that we must agree! I'm not only what I want to be; I'm also what people see in me. That's a great disadvantage. Sometimes I read in the reviews of my books that I'm part of a Jewish literary tradition, particularly the tradition of Shalom Aleichem. Yet I have never read so much as one page of Shalom Aleichem. All I know of him is the musical *Fiddler on the Roof.* I've seen the movie, but I've never read the book.

Personally, I don't understand how somebody can say *Jacob the Liar* is part of the Holocaust literature. It has to do with that, there's no doubt about it; it takes place where the Holocaust happened. But my impulse, my reason to write the book was not to write about the Holocaust. The result may be seen in this way, but I never intended to write a book about the Holocaust. I wrote a book about something that has to do with that theme, I can't deny it; but some Germanists, some literary theorists seem to be specializing in the Holocaust. What a horrible kind of imagination they must have.

It doesn't bother me when somebody categorizes this book as Holocaust literature. What bothers me is being called a Holocaust writer. That's not really what I am. This is the only book—maybe half of one other, too—that I wrote on that theme. Not because that theme doesn't interest me—I'm consumed by it—but I want to write about it only when I've found a good story.

*Yet, your book is rooted in the ghetto. At the end, the hero and the young girl closest to him are on their way to the death camp. What were you writing about, if not about the Holocaust?*

The reasons for a book have to lie in the present, not in the past. When I write a book, I must constantly ask myself why I'm doing it. What's the reason for writing this? I try to be guided by those present reasons. What rôle does hope play in the lives of people? What rôle can it play? Those are questions that bother me now, not in the past.

Hershel had never attracted attention until that time of praying, which led to the power failure, according to his conviction. Now he is making up for it. He is standing on the siding next to the freight car. The guards still haven't noticed him. Hershel is pressing his ear to the car side and is talking. I see him, pious Hershel, clearly moving his lips, listening, then speaking again. His brother, Roman, happens to be standing beside me, his eyes big as mill wheels. He is about to run over to Hershel to bring him back before it's too late. Two men have to hold him back by force and one has to whisper, "Stay quiet, you idiot, you yourself will draw their attention to him."

I can't hear what Hershel is saying and what those inside are telling him. The distance is much too great for that. But I can well imagine it and that has nothing to do with vague guesses. The more I think about it, the clearer do I know his words, although he never confirmed them.

"Hullo! Do you hear me?" says Hershel first off.

"We hear you," a voice from inside the car must have replied. "Who are you?"

"I'm from the ghetto," says Hershel then. "You have to hold on; only for a short while longer do you have to hold on. The Russians have already advanced past Bezanika!"

"How do you know that?" they ask from inside—everything quite logical and inevitable.

"You can believe me. We have a hidden radio. I have to leave now."

The confined express their gratitude unrestrainedly. A white dove has strayed over to them into the darkness. Their words are irrelevant. Perhaps they wish him good luck and riches and long life to a hundred and twenty before they hear his footsteps departing.

Stupefied, all of us are looking at Hershel who is wending his way back. Crackbrained as we are, we simply stand there and gawk instead of continuing to work and to act as if everything were quite ordinary. First we keep Roman from committing a great blunder, then we commit it ourselves. Maybe Hershel wouldn't have got away with it in any case. Who can know that after the fact? At any rate, we don't do anything that might divert them from him. Only now does he seem to discover fear. Until then everything had taken its own course, as if in accordance with unfathomable laws that somnambulists obey. His cover is more than insufficient, as good as non-existent. Hershel knows well why he is frightened. A pile of crates, an empty freight car further on, otherwise nothing in his path that he could really use for accompanying cover. I see him sticking his head around the corner of the car, centimeter after centimeter. He is already with us with his glances. I can already hear him tell about his trip around the world. Up to now his opposition has been quiet. The guard at the gate is standing with his back facing the railroad station area. Not a sound arouses his attention. The other two had disappeared, presumably into the house, where the rain had driven them. I see Hershel making his final preparations for his big sprint. I see him praying. Although he is still standing by the freight car and moving his lips, it is clearly evident that he isn't talking with those inside, but rather with his God. And then I turn my head to the guardhouse. It has a small attic window, which is open. On the window sill is a rifle that is being aimed in utter tranquility. I can't make out the man behind it. It's too dark in the room. I see only two hands adjusting the direction of the barrel until they are satisfied, then stopping as if modeled for a painting. What should I have done, I, who have never been a hero, what should I have done? If I were one, at best, shout. But what good would that have done? I do not shout. I close my eyes. An eternity passes. Roman says to me: "What are you closing your eyes for? Look, he'll make it, that crazy fellow!"

I don't know why at this moment I think of Chana, whom they shot to death in front of a tree, the name of which I don't know. I'm still thinking of her after the shot, until everyone around me is talking all at once. Just a single ordinary shot. The two hands had, as stated, plenty of time to prepare everything for the best possible advantage all through Hershel's prayer. It sounds strange. I've never heard a single shot, only several at once, as if a naughty child defiantly stamped its foot, or as if a balloon were blown up too violently and then burst, or even, since I'm now luxuriating in pictures, as if God had coughed. God coughed in Hershel's face.

Those locked in behind the reddish-brown sides might ask, "Say, there, what happened?"

Hershel is lying on his stomach between two rail ties across the track. His clenched right hand has fallen into a black puddle. His face, only half of which I can see at first, seems strange to me with the open eye. We are standing around him—this small break is not begrudged us—Roman bends down over him, pulling him away from the track, and turns him on his back. Then he takes off the fur cap. His fingers have difficulty unbuttoning the flaps under the chin. He puts the cap in his pocket and goes away. For the first time in this railroad station, Hershel's earlocks are allowed to blow free in the wind. Many of us have never seen them before and know them only from hearsay. So that's how Hershel Shtamm really looks without disguise. For the last time, his face bordered black from the wet earth and much hair. Someone closed his eyes. I won't lie; why should I? He wasn't handsome. He was very pious. He wanted to promote hope and died because of it.

In Jacob's head his self-reproaches open up lots of thoughts. He knows with horrifying preciseness what role he has played. You fabricate for yourself meager consolation. You imagine a large scale with two pans. On the one, you put Hershel; on the other, you pile up all the hope you have circulated among the people in the course of time. Which side will sink? The trouble is, you don't know how much hope weighs. No one will tell you. You have to find the formula alone and make the calculation alone. But you'll calculate in vain. The difficulties pile up; here's another: who is to tell you what harm has been prevented by your inventions? Ten catastrophes or twenty or even only a single one; what has been prevented will remain eternally hidden from you. Only what you have done is visible. It's lying there next to the track in the rain.

Even later, at noon, you haven't come any closer to the answer to the problem with the many unknown quantities. Off by himself, Jacob is spooning up his soup. Today, everyone leaves everybody else alone. He has avoided Roman Shtamm. Roman didn't look for him. Only at the wheelbarrow on which the tin bowls are placed after use they suddenly are standing opposite one another. They look each other in the eye, especially Roman. Jacob tells me: "He looked at me as if I had shot his brother."

The hours after work belong to Lena.
A while ago, Jacob had stopped in the vestibule in front of his door with her and had said: "Now pay attention, Lena, if something happens, so that you'll find the key to my room." He had said: "Here in back of the doorframe is a little hole in the wall; do you see? I'm sticking the key in now, and then the rock in front of it again. It is very easily removed. If you stand on tiptoes, you'll be tall enough. Try it." Lena tried it; she stretched, removed the rock, and with the greatest effort got the key, proudly showing it to Jacob. "Excellent," Jacob said, "note the spot well. I myself don't know why, but maybe it will be important someday. And one thing more, don't reveal the place to anyone."

I wanted to write a book about the value of story-telling; what it can do and what it cannot do. I wanted to write a book about lies. I had a story that I thought was worth telling. (It was different from the movie, a bit fantastic and a bit poetic maybe—it's difficult to speak about my own book that way.) There is comedy in it, and the comedy was very important, because it was a great challenge to find out if there is something that cannot be written about as a comedy. I wanted to find out.

And I was writing for readers who hadn't been there, who know these circumstances only from other books, or films, or TV—from books I don't like, from TV plays I don't like. I tried to open another door so they could get in touch with this period. All this may sound as if it's an attempt to write a special sort of Holocaust literature. Maybe the book is a part of that literature, but that was not my intention.

*You were not happy with the movie of your book. I must say I was quite moved by the film. You say that when you watch the movie as a spectator, you can enjoy it, but as the writer you are unhappy about it.*

As I said, it was important that I attempt to write a comedy—a sort of tragic comedy—and this was what got lost in the movie. I understand why it was done the way it was, but it is a pity. In the book, the narrator tells a story. That's quite a different thing from seeing that yellow star every minute of the whole movie. It has such weight it almost kills you.

*So you are saying that the movie loses the fantastical quality of the book, that it emerges as oppressive rather than having those lyrical moments of humour and wit that are liberating in the book.*

You said you were moved by the movie. That's the problem. The movie moves you too much, it bothers you too much. It doesn't make you free in a unique way: it doesn't make you able to fly, if you know what I mean. That's what I wanted the movie to do. It's not magic.

*You have said that you aren't happy with writers who are totally occupied with the Holocaust, and that some of the films and the literature about the Holocaust bother you. What is it that offends you when writers attempt to convey or depict the Holocaust?*

When I am writing a book, the important thing is the question, "Why am I doing this?" When I read some books about the Holocaust that have mountains of dead people in them, I ask myself why the writers are doing that. Why are they showing me that? It's important that literature have some effect. Writing a book is not like eating, it's not just a physical function. When I consider their reasons, I don't think they get the effect they probably want to have.

I read a sentence in a book by Jean-Paul Sartre that one dead person is a catastrophe, a thousand dead people are a number. It seems that this wisdom is too often forgotten. It's not enough just to be occupied with all that death. More important is the effect the books have. Now that we are living in a society that is sensitive enough that such things cannot happen any more, it seems to me almost unnecessary to be concerned about them.

When I return to Germany, there is going to be a big meeting of the trade unions for the fiftieth anniversary of the book burnings. They asked me if I would give a speech, and I agreed. Suddenly I thought, what shall I say to them? Shall I tell them it's not okay to burn books? What can I say on such an occasion? I searched a very long time for a present reason to speak about it. That is the answer to your question, I think. I will ask why we remember that day. What is the reason for meeting and remembering that fifty years ago the Nazis burned books? Just for remembrance? That's not enough for me. I am not interested in these memories; they are not so great—I can imagine better memories. It cannot be like looking at an insect under a magnifying glass, when there is no way out. The only important and good reason to remember is to ask ourselves what attitude was behind that happening, and where do we find that attitude today? That's a good reason to concern oneself with it. Just for remembrance? It's fruitless—and too many books about the Holocaust seem to me just for remembrance.

*You recently saw a couple of segments of a film called* Witness, *which involves one survivor after another recollecting what happened. You said that you had a curious response to it.*

Witness was just interviews with survivors of concentration camps. They told about what happened, and, for three hours, the camera focussed on just the heads of these people as they remembered. Some of them, naturally, were very moved, and cried when they spoke about those times. But something terrible happened to me: I was bored. I thought, "Oh, God, stop. I can't listen any more, I hear that so often." I know why they were moved, but it's impossible to translate that emotion to me; there's a limit.

Other survivors spoke about the times in a cool way, a sophisticated way. They told stories with effects and devices; they worked at what they were saying, and I was moved: they were cold but I was touched.

What I want to say is that it's not enough to be moved. There are some people, some victims, some survivors for whom it's enough. They have a button. You push on it, and their eyes fill up with tears. But they are not normal spectators, they are not normal readers—they are not normal people, they are survivors. I can understand that some authors want to create literature for the survivors. I don't want to do that.

I want to create literature for the others, not because there are more of them (it's not a business reason), but because I am more interested in them. It's not that I don't care about the survivors, but my interests are forward looking. I had a lot of trouble on this point with my father, for example. He was one of the survivors, and he had such a button. He always wanted a book or a film to push that button, so he would experience the right feeling—sorrow or pity. It was like a celebration for him, but it doesn't work for people in my generation, nor, I think, for those who are not survivors.

*So you write for an audience of the future.*

I write for me. I write what I want to, the way I want to. And maybe for other people who think and feel as I do.

*How did the German audience respond to* Jacob the Liar?

I can't say that there was a unanimous reaction. Some liked it and some didn't. I got the feeling that in the German Democratic Republic—in East Germany—there was a slightly different reaction than that in West Germany. It seemed to me that in East Germany it was seen as a period piece, a special story about a special time. In West Germany it was seen more as an allegory. The critics tried harder to interpret the book. I don't know who is right; sometimes I feel one way, sometimes the other. The mystery is that I don't know exactly what I am doing. I always try to discover it but I am not always successful.

*You've said that sometimes your books are more intelligent than you are.*

Maybe that's why I became a writer. Because sometimes—not always, unfortunately—I can go beyond a limit that I can't pass when I am talking or just thinking. The reasons are obvious. For example, I can't speak a sentence to you, in this specific situation, and then look at it, take it back, throw it away and speak a new one. What I have said, I've said; but what I have written is not published yet. I have to check it and I can write a better sentence.

When I rewrite a sentence, I keep in mind the alternatives I threw away. When a reader reads a sentence, it looks so strong, so sure; yet when I read it, I remember all the possibilities I didn't use, and I am not sure if I made the right decision. That's why I hate to reread my old work.

It sounds heartless, but for a writer it's essential to have a professional relation to what he is doing. As a writer, I am more interested in the story than in the event I am writing about. That doesn't mean that for me as a political person the event is unimportant; not at all. But my medium is stories, plots. I need them; without them I can't survive as a writer. You can't write with your heart: you write with your fingers and with your brain. If you forget, it will be revealed in your writing. I can't say how often I have failed because I have forgotten, but I try to keep some intellectual distance.

When the war was over I was seven years old, and I have forgotten almost everything. It's very strange, but I have no memories of the concentration camp. I have some memories of the ghetto before it, but not of the camp. I often ask myself why. Is it foolishness? Is it repression? I do not think so. The reason is that there was nothing to remember. I was a small child and small kids need a living environment, some intellectual stimulation in order to remember. Nobody cared for me, nobody had time to care for me. All my attention was concentrated on survival. I wasn't interested in discovering how the world works, I just wanted to find a piece of bread. One day was probably as grey as the next, and there is nothing to remember. The ghetto was alive—there was a community, family. I had friends. That's why I can remember so much more, even though I was much younger.

*Does the novel emerge from your own background?*

Not at all. It's an invented story, with a bit of real background.

*You mentioned that it evolved from a story your father told you, albeit in a different way.*

Once my father had accepted the fact that I was going to be a writer, which was a great disappointment for him, he told me he knew a man in the Lodz ghetto. He was a great hero. The man had a hidden radio, which was forbidden under penalty of death, and he listened to Radio London and other radio stations from foreign countries. He relayed hopeful news, which the people needed very much. One day the radio was discovered by the Germans, and they shot him.

My father said that the man was a great hero, and that I should write about him. Probably he thought the man needed a monument. I thought that the man had enough monuments in Holocaust literature and I felt no longing to write about him. Years later I thought again about this story, with one change: that man behaved the same way, but he did not have a radio. The other people in the ghetto just thought he had one. Now that, I thought, was a good idea for a story.

For me, probably the only one still alive and capable of having misgivings, that evening is the most incomprehensible in the entire story. Even when Jacob had explained it to me as well as he could, I didn't completely understand him. I asked Jacob, "Didn't you carry it too far? She could have betrayed you and everything would have been done for." "Oh, no," Jacob answered smiling, "Lena would never betray me." I said, "I mean completely unintentionally. A heedless word will slip out of a child's mouth. Somebody picks it up and builds an entire story out of it." "Lena weighs precisely what she says," Jacob answered, and I had to believe him. But there was something else that seemed hardly comprehensible to me. "There is something else, Jacob. You couldn't be certain that she didn't see through everything. How easily she could have noticed what was really happening. She is a clever girl, as you yourself say. Wasn't it fantastic luck that she didn't see through it?" "She saw through it," Jacob said, and his eyes became quite proud. . . .

Let's listen to that evening.

A great deal of excitement. Lena is hanging on to Jacob's coat. The cellar corridor is long and gloomy. The metal doors they pass by on tiptoe are all locked, as if they had inestimable riches to hide. The air is damp and cold despite the month of August outside. In concerned anticipation Jacob insisted upon a winter dress, stockings, and scarf for Lena. On the ceiling and walls droplets are hanging and glistening like weak light bulbs.

"Are you afraid?"

"No," she whispers decisively, and that's not too much of a lie.

"Where do you have the radio?"

"You'll endure it a bit longer."

He squats in front of her, takes her chin in one hand, turns her face to himself so that no glance goes astray and begins with the most necessary preparations: "Listen exactly to what I tell you. First, you must promise me that you'll be good and do everything I now ask of you. Sacred word of honor?"

The sacred word of honor, used only at quite important occasions, is given impatiently. Her eyes demand him not to dwell so long upon preliminaries.

"You'll remain sitting here very quietly. The radio is behind that wall there. I'm going there now to turn it on, then it'll play and we'll both hear it. But if I see you stand up, I'll turn it off again immediately."

"Can't I see it?"

"By no means!" says Jacob decisively. "You're not even allowed to hear it either when you're so little. That's strictly forbidden. But I'll make an exception in your case. Agreed?"

What can she do? She is being blackmailed and has to give in. Listening is better than nothing, even though she had promised herself the direct view. Besides, she could, she could . . . we'll find out.

"What's your radio playing?"

"I don't know that ahead of time. I have to turn it on first."

The preparations are concluded. No more can be done for your own security. Jacob stands up, goes to the wall, stops at the opening, and looks at Lena once more with looks that should bind her as far as possible to the bedstead. Then he disappears finally.

Jacob's eyes must first get accustomed to the new light. It hardly extends behind the partition. His foot stumbles against the pail full of holes.

"Was that the radio?"

"No, not yet. It'll take another moment."

"It's starting," says Jacob, prepared for the first thing that comes out.

A fingernail plunks against the pail; that's how radios are turned on. Then the air is full of humming and whistling. The warming-up time is skipped; that particular is reserved for connoisseurs. Jacob's radio has right from the start the proper temperature. The choice of station is also quickly accomplished. An announcer in a high-pitched voice, as stated, the first thing that comes out, proclaims: "Good evening, ladies and gentlemen, near and far. You will now hear an interview with the English prime minister, Sir Winston Churchill." The speaker then hands over the microphone. A man in a middle voice-range can be heard. The reporter: "Good evening, Sir Winston."

Then Sir Winston himself, in a very deep voice and clearly foreign intonation: "Good evening, everyone." . . .

A fingernail plunks against the pail. That's how radios are turned off. Jacob wipes the perspiration from his forehead. A bit weak that interview, he thinks, and also a bit over Lena's head. But you're not—unfortunately, that will never change—a Sholem Aleichem in inventiveness. Don't demand too much from a tormented man I hope it will suffice for today. Jacob appears again. It turns out that things are going splendidly not only in the region of Bezanika but also not any worse here in the cellar. Lena has finally heard a radio with her own ears, strictly forbidden for children, and is fascinated. It could have happened differently, too. To mask your voice was an innovation, moreover, three different kinds at once. Lena could have also coldly demanded that he stop the nonsense now and finally turn on the radio. That would have been a blow to Jacob, even the thought of it, but she wouldn't even dream of such words. Everything is as nice as could be. He sees that immediately.

"Did you like it?"

"Yes."

Mutual satisfaction. Jacob is standing in front of her and is about to talk of leaving: we've all had our fun; your bed is waiting; but Lena says: "It isn't over yet, is it?"

"Why, of course."

"I'd like to hear more."

"No, no, enough for now," he says, but he says it only feebly. A short dispute: it's late already; Lena would like to hear more; perhaps another time; just a little bit; never satisfied; just turn the radio on again; she'll be happy with everything. Jacob sneezes again. On this evening the whole world has the sneezes. While wiping his nose he examines her expression and finds no suspicion. That is the deciding factor.

"What do you want to hear?"

Well, Jacob is once again sitting on the pail completely silent, gradually overcome by ambition. By ambition concerning the brass band. That thought gives him no peace although it has been silent for a good forty years and covered with dust and the instruments rusty. Jacob wants to try it, resolved as he is today.

In the beginning is the plunk, then humming and whistling. The second time around it sounds more skilled. Then it starts full blast, the music, with drum and cymbals to which the first measure belongs. Drum and cymbals are followed by a solitary trombone that needs several notes to get on the right track. The melody is uncertain, Jacob says. An improvised melodic line, interspersed with diverse familiar themes, but devoid of any regular tempo. What is clear is that it's some sort of march. His feet timidly take over the percussion, supported by his fingers which make use of the pail, thereby freeing his mouth for the rest of the instruments. A single trombone does not yet produce a brass band. It must be alternated with the trumpet and that, in turn, with the falsetto clarinet, and every now and then a tuba blast from the bottom of your throat. Jacob loses, as they say, all his inhibitions. . . . The cellar resounds with sounds never yet heard. Perhaps, too much effort for a child like Lena who would be satisfied even with less elaborate material. But let me remind you, ambition is at stake, a voluntary test, and mastery thrives best without constraint. Soon the proper tone is achieved without difficulty. Trumpets and trombones throw each other phrases back and forth, practice variations, and almost always bring it off successfully. The clarinet is necessarily pushed to the background more and more, too unnatural a register, while the tuba can be heard more and more often, from time to time even undertaking a little showpiece of its own, a succession of notes in the lower registers, and when the breath gives out, taking refuge in drumming on the pail for two or three measures.

In a phrase, a piece of music history is being written. Jacob is a clamoring success. Lena is brought to her feet from the bedstead. She stands up inaudibly, forgotten are all the sacred words of honor. Her legs slink unopposed to the partition. She has to see the thing that sounds so much like Jacob and yet very differently, that can speak in various voices, sneeze as he does, and make such peculiar noises. Lena carefully stretches her head around the corner invisible to Jacob who is sitting not only sideways, but also keeping his eyes tightly shut, a sign of the greatest mental and physical effort. Oblivious to the world, he is making noises in accordance with rules known only to him. No, Jacob doesn't notice that he has been sitting naked and unguarded for several moments. Afterward, only one question remains. She will inquire as to whether he has another radio besides this one. Presumably he doesn't; otherwise, where would he keep it hidden if not here? Lena knows what no one knows. She sits down again quietly on her spot. Her pleasure in listening has not diminished, just mixed with a few thoughts that are nobody's business.

Then the march is over, but not yet the performance. When Jacob reappears exhausted and delighted and with a withered mouth, Lena tempestuously demands an encore—all good things come in threes and now truly so! That proves to him she has not suspected anything. That was also proof enough, he thinks; if this march went well, then nothing more can happen to him.

"But this is the very last one!" says Jacob.

He sets out again for his broadcasting room, his next program already in mind, and plunks. Lena is quite lucky. Jacob soon finds the radio station where fairy tales are told by a kind fellow who says, "For all the children who are listening to us, the storyteller will tell the tale about the sick princess."

He has a voice similar to that of Sir Winston Churchill, just as deep but somewhat softer, and yet without a foreign intonation.

"Do you know that one?" asks Jacob as Jacob.

"No. But how come there is a storyteller on the radio?"

"What do you mean, how come? There just is."

"But you said the radio is forbidden for children. And aren't fairy tales only for children?"

"That's correct. But I meant it's forbidden for us in the ghetto. Where there is no ghetto, children are allowed to listen. And there are radios everywhere. Clear?"

"Clear."

# George Segal

ALLAN FINKELMAN

Painter and sculptor George Segal was born in New York City in 1924. He graduated from New York University and was granted an honorary Doctorate of Fine Arts from Rutgers University. He presently lives in New Jersey with his wife and two children.

Since the mid-1950s he has had almost annual one-man shows, and has taken part in as many as ten group shows a year. His work has been shown in and purchased by private collections and public art galleries around the world: New York, Paris, Washington, Zurich, Munich, Brussels, Jerusalem, London, Helsinki, Chicago, Venice, Sao Paulo, Tokyo, Dusseldorf and Stockholm, to name a few. His work is the subject of four books, published in the United States, Germany and Spain.

There is something strangely innocent about George Segal; an extraordinary loyalty to truth, freedom and The American Way.

He was quite the most conversational of the interviewees, utterly earnest, eager and homespun. Segal is so lacking in pretension that somehow the words take on a simple, unself-conscious strength. His sculptures, and their unusual technique, both mirror, I believe, the unrelenting honesty of the man.

---

*Mr. Segal, it is difficult on radio to get a visual sense of the sculpture you have created as a memorial to the Holocaust; do you think you could try to describe it?*

The sculpture consists of eleven life-size white-plaster figures. Ten dead bodies lie on a floor in a disorganized, dishevelled heap. There is a single male figure standing behind a barbed-wire fence with one hand on the wire, the other hand just dangling. I looked at about a thousand photographs before I started working, and I tried to make the sculpture, which occupies a space about twenty feet by twenty feet, resemble my memory of those black-and-white photographs of the camps in 1945—when everybody heard about the awfulness of what was happening in Auschwitz, Bergen-Belsen, and the other death camps that the Germans had been running. I had heard about these camps since the early 1940s from my parents, who are Jewish. But it was long-distance, non-personal involvement. My father was the only member of his family who had come to the United States. He had seven brothers, none of whom survived.

I did not want to work on this sculpture. I had refused for about six months, because I knew I would have to saturate myself in death. But I promised that I would at least see the site and talk about it.

I was in Tokyo with my wife installing a show when the Israelis invaded Lebanon. I knew nothing of the war or its origins, since I don't understand Japanese. We landed in San Francisco, checked into a hotel, turned on the TV, and for the first time in my life I heard anti-Semitic noise coming out of the American tube. I had been born and raised in America, and in light of the enormity of the Holocaust, this was inconceivable. I decided then and there to make the piece.

*Do you mean you had lived your entire life in the United States without hearing or encountering anti-Semitism?*

The anti-Semitism I had encountered was veiled, elusive, nowhere near the stories of the *Kristalnacht* or being beaten up in the streets because you were a Jewish kid; nowhere near the decision to annihilate an entire people that the Germans put into practice. America really was innocent in comparison to what the Germans had practised.

*What was it that you heard that day that so riveted you?*

I think it was American reporters irritated at the Israeli military censorship, and also the naïveté of the American reporters repeating the PLO claims. I had been to that part of the world, and I knew how small the cities were. Yet they were reporting casualties in Sidon and other Lebanese cities that were larger than the entire population. Something was out of kilter. I retain an innocent faith in ideas of American freedom and democracy, and my family has lived freely expressing its Jewishness all these years. I was shocked.

My father was a Russian Jew; he was a poultry farmer, and he was innocently patriotic about America. The community of Jewish farmers was about fifty per cent German-Jewish refugees, smart enough to have read the handwriting on the wall and to get out. They told us stories about German behaviour. After the war my father sent me to a couple that had survived the camps. They were trying to start a poultry farm. He sent me to teach them how to handle the machinery and how to feed the chickens. They told me stories that were incredibly inhuman: the woman had been carrying her baby in her arms; an attack dog had been trained to leap and savagely bite the throats of babes in arms. Now that's a bit more drastic than a sarcastic remark, don't you think?

*You don't have any difficulty persuading me.*

*You said that you looked at about a thousand photographs that were taken during liberation of the camps, and the photographs gave you the inspiration for your motif.*

A survivor whom I had been introduced to told me, "Drop all your intellectual nonsense"—he didn't say nonsense, but he implied it, correctly—"a monument like this has to make people cry." He was perfectly right. The more I looked at photographs, the more obscene the disorderly dumping and heaping of dead bodies became.

Any time anybody dies, in any culture, there is an order of grieving and religious observance. The body is laid out; the family weeps; a religious person talks about mortality and vanity and a larger picture. There's an orderliness to the repeated ritual of a funeral.

The arrogant, callous disregard, the chaotic dumping of human bodies in these photographs revolted me. That disorder was in such sharp contrast to everything that I had been brought up to respect in European art and culture and human values: the order of the golden mean, the precision and balance of the Greeks. It made a mocking irony of Beethoven and Mozart and Bach.

*You therefore captured this antithesis in your sculpture. I gather you used real people and did the casts with them.*

Yes. I could have used corpses. I chose not to because it's now forty years after the fact, and I wanted a chance to deal on several levels. There is the necessity of the first shock of revulsion; it has to look convincing enough to disturb you when you look at it. But after you look at the sculpture for a while, it also becomes necessary to think about human things: tender gestures, or gestures of regard, gestures of humanity. I had to use live people playing dead.

*Was it—forgive the naïveté of this—a traumatic experience to arrange human beings in shapes and processes that were brutalizing and dehumanizing, in order to evoke what you wanted to evoke?*

Very much. I must say that my models were marvellous—sensitive, intelligent people who understood exactly. I made very clear to them what I was trying to do, and that I needed their help; and they free-associated their ideas of death to me while I was covering them with plaster. It was amazing, our American innocence. Most of my models had not seen a dead body; we didn't know when rigor mortis sets in. We were innocently play-acting a great deal of the time.

After we agreed on a pose, I dipped plaster-impregnated bandages in water and put them on my model. In a very few minutes, the plaster bandages dry—the model has to hold still until that happens—and then I pop the pieces off. Later I reassemble the pieces and construct an entire figure in stronger plaster.

In order to make some reference to the specific Jewish nature of it, I buried two Old Testament images in the heap of bodies. One was Adam and Eve, the other was Abraham and Isaac. I showed the man who posed for Abraham a picture postcard of Donatello's sculpture of that theme. He recoiled in horror at the way Abraham was grabbing the hair of Isaac. He said, "A real father who loved his son would never grab his son like that, even at the moment of being ready and willing to sacrifice him. He would cover his eyes." Whether he said that in conscious or unconscious memory of Rembrandt's etching of the same theme, I don't know; but I admired his humanity, expressing his regard for the child, even as he was about to kill him. So I introduced something of the complexity of this Old Testament image in a collapsed version into this dead heap of bodies.

*How exactly did you work in the Abraham and Isaac image? It's a favourite image of yours, isn't it?*

The only thing that would be left would be a remnant of an essential gesture. Both bodies are on the floor. The little boy's hands are behind his back, the act of being bound, and one hand of Abraham protectively shields his face.

*With regard to the other image,* The New York Times *quotes you as saying, "I became as interested in Eve's sensuality as anything else. It has to do with survival." But Eve is dead in your representation, Mr. Segal.*

Quite so, quite so. Eve is resting her head on Adam's stomach, right next to his rib, and she has a half-eaten apple in her hand. Yes, she does radiate sensuality and sexuality. I thought it necessary to introduce that level into the piece, which is about my revulsion at this obscene act: look at the vast universe that's lost in this kind of insane killing.

*In what way does it speak to survival if the symbolic representation of survival is annihilated?*

All of us raised in the United States are taught ideas of freedom, democracy and civilized behaviour that come from western Europe, regardless of our religion. All religions talk of a basis of morality. We're taught respect for civilized order. If we don't make ourselves and our children aware of some dark underside of human nature, a fever of insanity can run through a modern industrial state. Any modern industrial state has this enormous capacity for the efficient destruction of enormous numbers of people. Unless we say something about the value of individuals, the devastating loss of a single person, unless there's a reflex, a recoil of horror, we're all in danger of death.

*For the one standing figure, which gives the work a focus, you used an actual survivor.*

That's right. A close friend, someone whom I enormously respect. He is Dutch; he was a young boy when he survived the camps, and he made his way to Israel. He's young, vigorous, in perfect physical condition; yet as he posed for me, he kept sinking deeper and deeper into a state of hopeless despair that was very moving. His state of mind made him seem to age before my eyes.

*You have said that the central figure had to be a survivor because you felt that certain things had to be authentic. You were, I take it, grappling with representation, on one hand, and the need to get to the truth, on the other.*

I dodge behind a famous quote of Picasso's. "Art is a lie that tells the truth." Obviously, I walk a dangerous tightrope between realism and state of mind. I think that my work needs a certain amount of realism to make a situation or a place visually convincing. But I'm also interested in how to put thoughts or attitudes into the piece and make them clear enough for people to recognize. If I was going to do reality, I would put smell in, I would put flesh colour, I would put decayed flesh. I think that would just induce vomit or fright, and that's not what an art work is intended to do. If this is to be a memorial to the Holocaust, it has to invoke vividly what happened, but it also has to be a container for thoughts, feelings, reactions.

*You are trying to come to grips visually with something that many people, even in literature, have shied away from. You're not uncomfortable with that, I take it.*

No. I insist on using a realistic basis, and yet I'm unwilling to become totally realistic. I walk around like a pair of disembodied eyes. I see things beyond the surface of my skin; that's the outside visual world; and I have sensations—of light and heat and smell and touch—and all that is outside the boundaries of my body. Yet I'm forever aware of my own thoughts and forever thinking; I'm having reactions and making judgements; I'm distilling my experience and trying to make some sense out of it.

As innocently as possible, that's how I can describe the quality of my own experience. As directly as I can, that's how I try to make my art.

I have no quarrel with abstraction: my teachers were abstractionists. I admire it enormously. A long list of ideas in art and science, philosophy and religion, is based on abstraction; but those abstractions are always based on receiving information from your senses. It's that peculiar combination that I think is necessary.

However, I have been critical of a trend of thinking in abstract art that becomes more and more divorced from literary subject-matter or the experience of the real world. I've felt for a long time that it should be possible to restore to art the passion of strongly felt subject-matter, that art can be more than a collection of beautiful forms placed in utopian order. The hunt for the universal—this relentless hunt that every intelligent group of people has—should be based on the particular and the specific, on close observance of the outside visual world, very much the way science has always worked. You examine the real world, and you arrive at a true perception after that. So it's important for me to deal with specific individuals and real objects.

*How is the public reacting to the memorial sculpture?*

People are coming with their families and are walking around hushed, as if they are in a very private space. I'm taking that as a high compliment.

*Have you heard that they feel a little discomfited at the effort to encapsulate in sculpture an event of such enormity?*

I think that's irrelevant.

*Tell me why. There is so much apprehension in the Jewish community, so many who feel that the evocation of the Holocaust in merely one dimension or one fashion or one incident can diminish it.*

You're quoting Elie Wiesel. He has spoken often of the enormity of the Holocaust and the impossibility of any aesthetic or artistic representation doing justice to it. Yet he's obsessed, himself. Mr. Wiesel is a brilliant spokesman for internal feeling, and my first tendency would be to agree with what he says. Yet, between six and seven hundred thousand people died in the German siege of Leningrad. When I visited, four years ago, the Russians were talking about the Germans and World War Two as if it had happened yesterday.

There are two hundred million people living in the United States. If the United States had suffered casualties of a hundred million in 1945, we would still be talking about that horror. We simply can't grasp the enormity of fifty per cent casualties, or the enormity of the decision of a modern industrial state to annihilate all the Jews in the world. And yet it is not the sole property of the survivors of that experience. It can happen again, unless civilized people everywhere become revolted. This experience has to become everybody's property. I think that artists are the antennae of a community. Not everybody can express this; only the people that have the language and the sensibility can express what everybody feels, which is why we hunt for artists. But the consciousness has to be universal.

# Annette Insdorf

VOLKER HINZ

Annette Insdorf was born in Paris. She grew up in New York and was educated at Queens and Yale Universities. Since 1975, Insdorf has been an associate professor of English at Yale, where she teaches film history and criticism. She held previous university teaching posts at the New School, Fordham and at Columbia. She is also a translator, lecturer and moderator, and hosts a weekly television programme on the cinema.

She is a frequent contributor to *The New York Times, Arts and Leisure*, and her articles and criticism have appeared in many film journals, as well as in *Rolling Stone, Newsday, The San Francisco Chronicle* and *The Los Angeles Times*. Insdorf is the author of two book-length studies: *François Truffaut* (1979), and *Indelible Shadows: Film and the Holocaust* (1983), for which she was granted a Rockefeller Foundation Fellowship.

With Annette Insdorf, it quickly became apparent that it's just not possible to convey film adequately on radio. As a result, this was perhaps the most difficult interview of all. Our conversation necessarily became a survey of Holocaust cinema rather than an analysis of cinematic content. Perhaps when so much is visual, it's impossible to do otherwise. Nonetheless, I think that some useful points were made simply because of the sweep of Insdorf's knowledge and authority.

---

*Your book,* Indelible Shadows, *is given largely to exposition, rather than to judgements, pejorative, lyrical or otherwise. Did you have a reason for that?*

Absolutely. My feeling was that I should try to be a translator in the best sense of the term. Cinema is images and sounds and things that can't always be articulated verbally; but I wanted people reading my book to be able to envision the film, to desire to see the film or, if they had already seen it, to be able to recall the images that I was discussing. I also felt that my rôle was not necessarily judgemental. I often define my critical rôle not as a reviewer, but rather as someone who tries to engage the reader in intelligent discussion. I don't like to tell people, hey, this is a bad film, this is a good film, go see it, don't see it. That's the job for people who have two minutes on television. I've been a professor for about ten years, and I like to turn my students on to what I think are good films, important or interesting films, and then to allow them to fight back. I like to mention something, and then have them put in their image or idea.

*At one point you quote Elie Wiesel, saying that his sense of the Holocaust is untranslatable into words. Does that extend to film as well?*

I feel that cinema is a very young art, compared to painting and literature and music, and we have not yet finished developing the form of cinematic vocabulary. I have seen too many fine films that have succeeded in conveying some of the horror, some of the resistance, some of the complexity of the Holocaust to believe that the film medium is incapable of doing justice to the historical event.

I do, however, acknowledge that when a film is being made within a commercial context—whether it's Hollywood, American television, or even European mass-market films— the commercial exigencies of the box office make it very hard to deal appropriately with the Holocaust, or any serious subject. I don't think that Vietnam, for example, has been treated with great depth or intelligence in films. It's very hard to make good films about difficult themes; but I think it's possible, and I think that, increasingly, technological developments are giving good film-makers a greater vocabulary to work with.

You can't do a nice soap opera of the Holocaust with a beginning and a middle and an end. That's wrong, because you give people an easy cathartic experience, easy tears or indignation, and then they go home again. I'm interested in films that make you feel uncomfortable, because one of the goals of film is to make you come to grips with something that you would not have seen otherwise, not to divert you and send you home smiling.

I can appreciate that Elie Wiesel's been offended. He has the right to be; he is a survivor. I was fortunate enough never to have been near Auschwitz, although my parents are survivors. I approached the Holocaust first as a film historian and critic, aware of the limitations within which films are made these days. I honestly believe that even the films that I criticized for being simplistic, like NBC's *Holocaust*, are well intentioned. These films have had a positive influence on audiences—young people, for example, who didn't know anything about the Holocaust before they saw the program— and on film-makers who, upon seeing NBC's *Holocaust*, felt the need to do better. In other words, even when a film is not great in its own terms, it is an important part of an ongoing debate in the making of films about the Holocaust.

*When gas-chamber episodes are neatly packaged between commercials for deodorants, is it not almost mutilation for an historical event to be subject to such commercial crudity?*

Yes. You've quoted part of my attack on *Holocaust* and I believe every word of that. At the same time, what is the alternative? Do I prefer *Holocaust* on NBC to nothing? This was one question I had to raise for myself all along the way. Here's where Elie Wiesel and I have occasionally disagreed. We've discussed this a number of times, he and I, and he is leading me increasingly to see his point of view. I believe that we have to guard against these simplifications, that we have to question them, denounce them if necessary and support the good versions. And yet, when I spoke to a lot of my students between the ages of eighteen and twenty-two at Yale University, many of them, believe it or not, had never heard the word "Auschwitz" before. Perhaps they've heard the word, but never within a context that gave it any meaning.

I would prefer my students' first encounter with the images of Auschwitz to be *Night and Fog* or any fine documentary film. But I know that that's very unrealistic. If *Night and Fog* were shown on television tonight, it would receive maybe two per cent of the audience that would watch *Holocaust.* I'm just acknowledging the realities of the film industry and of mass-market phenomena. I guess I'm still optimistic enough to believe that films like *Holocaust* ultimately do more good than harm. They make the Holocaust something that people are interested in: perhaps people will go to see more and better films about it. Perhaps they will lead film-makers to make better films about it.

*What do you think of* Sophie's Choice? *I judge that your book was written before the film was released.*

It was. However, I have recently added three paragraphs or so to the end of the chapter called "The Hollywood Version of the Holocaust." This film really cried out for inclusion, since my book would be published a few months after it. My feeling about *Sophie's Choice* is admiring and respectful, despite my distance from some other Hollywood attempts. I must confess, however, that I saw it before reading the novel. The next day I began reading the novel, and when I finished I went back and saw the film again. I had held off on reading Styron's book. I did not want to have to ask, "Was it faithful?" but simply, "Was it a good film?"

I should preface what I'm saying with one other statement. I don't think *Sophie's Choice* is a Holocaust film. Nor do I think that the novel is a Holocaust novel. The events are all narrated, and therefore mediated, by the voice of Stingo, alias Styron. Sophie herself is seen only insofar as Stingo perceives her, loves her, attempts to understand her. For me, the Auschwitz sequences in *Sophie's Choice* are always mediated both by Stingo's perspective and by Sophie's subjective voice and image.

I'll try to explain why this is important. It's one thing to show Auschwitz and claim that it's objective reality: a colour film begins and you see Auschwitz. I find that very difficult, depressing and wrong, because it is somehow suggesting that this is *it*. When a film shows Auschwitz only through the subjective recollection of one character, and acknowledges that it is the distorted and hazy recollection of one person, it has an honesty about it that I appreciate.

The Auschwitz sequences in *Sophie's Choice* are always in a kind of sepia, black-and-white tone. They're bracketed from the rest of the film; they don't look real. Secondly, the sequences begin with a close-up of Sophie's face, and she's kind of drunk. You hear her voice narrating, and every so often you return to a close-up of her face while this Auschwitz material is being presented. This is a very subtle thing, but I think it's Alan Pakula's attempt to remind us of the subjectivity of what we're seeing—it's not Auschwitz, but Sophie's

Auschwitz. This may seem very minor, but I think a lot of Hollywood films have not had that narrative honesty.

I also think that it could have been a really "Hollywood" film. It could have had manipulative, emotional music soaring on the soundtrack whenever something happened. It could have had simplistic bad guys and good guys. It also could have had very self-conscious camera movements, which would make it one of those technological zippy films you see these days from the young directors. Instead I think it was very sensitive and intelligent in its direction.

I grant you that the film doesn't come near the complexity of the novel. When you adapt a film from a six-hundred-page novel, you have to compress and you sometimes have to cut things that give the story its real meaning. I wish that the film could have included Stingo's ongoing meditation about slavery, his attempt to place Auschwitz in the context of oppression on a wider scale, perhaps, or different images of oppression. We don't get that in the film, so people say, hey, this is a Holocaust movie. If you read the novel, you understand it's not exactly that. It's about a writer trying to come to grips with evil in the twentieth century, and with his love for a survivor.

*You will admit, however, that for the great mass of human-kind who know* Sophie's Choice, *either as novel or film, it is a depiction of the Holocaust. It would be a revelation to them to see it merely as one writer's grappling with evil. It is more likely, and I think fairly, to be seen as a Holocaust novel. Here is Sophie, survivor of the Holocaust, whose choice—the heart of the novel—occurred on the platform at Auschwitz.*

The title is not "Sophie's Choice at Auschwitz." It's a more ambiguous title. On the first level it is meant to be about a choice she makes between two children, but the title is vague, and the novel ends with choice between living and dying. I see that the title has resonance on many levels. I'm not speaking necessarily as the child of survivors, or as an ordinary feeling person who walks into a movie theatre or picks up a novel; but I think that part of my job is to pick out the small ways that a film-maker can render a difficult task intelligible and admirable. When I learned that Alan Pakula would be directing *Sophie's Choice* I prepared myself for exactly what I saw: impeccable handling of actors, restrained story-telling, and a distance from the immediate horror of the material, in order to let your intelligence work, too.

*What threw me about the film, in particular, were the transport segments. In reality, those trains never arrived with people stepping easily onto the platform. They were always crowded with the dead. Many, many people died en route in those freight cars. In the descriptions by survivors, these platform scenes were never a restrained marching in groups. There were beatings, shootings, screams and terror, and all of the chaos of consigning people to the right and to the left. If the depiction of an event of such enormity is reduced to a mere interlude, maybe it's better not to show it at all.*

I have two responses to that. The transports that had Jews in them were not exactly the same as the transports that held political prisoners. From the deportation to the outcome at Auschwitz, Nazis always made a distinction between Jews and other prisoners. Jews were treated as cattle, lice, insects— I'm using some of the terminology from the Nazi accounts. And, of course, one major problem is that *Sophie's Choice* chooses to focus on a Catholic Polish woman and not a Jew. There were Catholic Polish women who died at Auschwitz, and some who survived, but the specificity of the Holocaust *viz à viz* Jewish victims is perhaps what should be stressed in films and novels, because that is more factually correct.

I suspect that if Pakula shows the arrival in Auschwitz with a certain calm, it's not because he's trying to take away the horror, or doesn't know that the horror was there. I know Pakula viewed *Night and Fog, Kitty Returned to Auschwitz*—countless Holocaust films. He read a lot of material before making the film, and was very scared about being unfaithful to the event. But if he had had chaos, screaming and gunshots, the horror of Auschwitz would have been the typical one that we see in films, a nameless, arbitrary, loud, screaming horror.

What he does instead is make the horror a question posed with the most polite civility in a quiet tone of voice: "Choose which child will live." To me that horror is greater than the screaming, within the narrative terms of *Sophie's Choice*. It derives part of its urgency from the calm in which it is said. I think that Pakula is trying to suggest that the Nazis were very educated and intelligent human beings who were able to quote Goethe, and be "religious," yet ask a prisoner to choose one child over another. It's a different kind of horror that he's placing in relief.

*You say that* Night and Fog *is the best of the concentration-camp films. Without stressing too much its precise content—I don't know whether radio can convey it—why do you feel the documentary form is so valid here?*

I don't consider *Night and Fog* a pure documentary. It is more a poetic meditation on Auschwitz that uses documentary material. I've praised most of the documentaries in my book for one or two reasons. Some are simple and straightforward, and therefore searing in their immediacy. *Kitty Returned to Auschwitz* is a film made for British television, in which a survivor returns to the scene with her son, now a doctor, and explains to him what happened there, her life there. She is an extraordinary human being on camera. She gets carried away with her passionate recollections but always is able lucidly to articulate what happened. The camera simply follows her. That, to me, is a great film.

*The Sorrow And The Pity* is also a great film, partly through its ability to juxtapose interviews with different people. The result is complex panorama of what the French were like during World War Two. It's a frightening film, for it does not show the French as they like to think of themselves, as having been active resisters. It shows that, by and large, they were passive collaborators.

*Night and Fog* is a third type, which I call the personal documentary.Here the camera is an active presence that investigates rather than merely records images. It moves through the bunkers of present-day Auschwitz, the places where people slept, the crematoria, insistently showing it to us, in all its dimensions. The act of the camera represents the film-makers trying to move in and penetrate something. Then, very often, the camera will stop, and you go to archival footage, which is an acknowledgement that, within the present, even when you go to the very end of the camp, you can't really see what happened. The camera is telling me something. *Night and Fog* uses real footage and the narration of a survivor. The real thing is more scary and more noble, I guess, than the fictional attempts.

There have also been superb fiction films, which have utilized cinematic language to create horror, to create courage, to create sympathy. I believe that fiction can and must rise to the occasion. My experience, though, in watching films that deal with the Holocaust, is that those that affected me most profoundly and which I tend to show in my classes over and over again are documentaries—first *Night and Fog* and then *The Witnesses*.

I've just seen one called *The Gathering*. It shows about six survivors telling their stories to the camera. The impact of this oral history, of this testimony, is shattering. You cannot compare that experience with watching Gregory Peck as Dr. Mengele in *The Boys From Brazil*.

*I was interested to read that the film* Lili Marleen *was tremendously popular because, though it didn't exonerate the Germans, it treated them as good Germans. What has happened to the German cinema in response to the Holocaust?*

*Lili Marleen* was the number-one box-office hit in Germany, and it did pretty well in France. Nevertheless, I see it as an atypical German response to the Holocaust. *Lili Marleen* was an insidious film; it's the only film that I outrightly attack in my book. The main reason I attacked it is *because* it was the number-one hit in Germany. Had it passed by relatively unnoticed, I would have said, well, here's Fassbinder doing his number, only with the Holocaust instead of the post-war Germany of Maria Braun.

Fortunately, the other German films that I've seen have been noble attempts to come to grips with the suppressed legacy of the Holocaust. This was a subject that was not dealt with in cinema, or in literature, in classrooms, in churches. People did not talk about what had gone on between 1939 and 1945.

I am sometimes indulgent about NBC's *Holocaust*, because it was one of the things that unleashed German consciousness, self-awareness. I was in Europe when it was shown in 1979, and I remember the reports out of Berlin and Munich. People were suddenly using the word "Holocaust," which hadn't been used in thirty-five years. Film-makers, especially young ones, started thinking about their responsibility to unearth this legacy of guilt, of complicity, of passivity—whatever term you use—and also to find the stories of Germans who had resisted.

This afternoon, I am going to a screening of *The White Rose*. This is a German film about people who tried to assassinate Hitler. We have to know about them, as well as about the lousy Germans. I've seen a number of films by young German film-makers attempting to investigate the past and to commemorate the good Germans. These are very important additions to the body of work on the Holocaust.

*What about* Our Hitler?

*Our Hitler* cannot be categorized. It exists only within its own terms, which are phantasmagorical and theatrical and stylized and outrageous and difficult, and occasionally boring and occasionally brilliant. As with any film that is seven and a half hours long, there are parts that you want to throw tomatoes at and parts when you want to fall asleep, and parts that you want to take notes about, and parts that you want to cheer.

*Our Hitler* is a very strange film. It has an inherent problem: it is aimed at a very small audience. Here's Annette Insdorf, the populist, the occasional defender of Hollywood, speaking; here's the film professor who tries to use the cinema to touch large groups of people. *Our Hitler* has much more to do with Syberberg's obsessive nightmares and fantasies and addiction to Wagner, and with cinematic self-consciousness, than with any reality of Adolf Hitler.

Personally I much prefer Syberberg's film *The Confessions of Winifred Wagner*, a documentary he made before *Our Hitler*. It's a rather straightforward interview with Winifred Wagner, in which she self-justifies every few seconds. Every now and then Syberberg includes a voice-over or a title that contradicts what she's saying. Now, for me, that kind of film is better in terms of the Holocaust than *Our Hitler*, which brings together many disparate theatrical devices and little fragments of perception, but ultimately is quite pretentious.

By the way, I always go on record as saying that these films must be made, must be seen. You can't just make films for the mass audience. But when I think about *Our Hitler*, which should, perhaps, be seen by Germans, and by Americans, and by the French, I don't know too many who would sit there for seven and a half hours, let alone watch Hitler's valet speaking for twenty minutes about Hitler's underwear.

Basically, I would defend *Our Hitler* against its detractors, but it was with some resistance that I included it in my book on films on the Holocaust. As with *Sophie's Choice*, I have to take a step back and say that it is not about the Holocaust the way *Night and Fog* is about the Holocaust. It is about a certain aspect of the German mentality, German romanticism, which is inseparable from the Holocaust but which cannot be taken as a comprehensive analysis of what happened.

*Do you sense that, on balance, German films have been more critical of German participation than self-justifying?*

The only film that I can think of that showed the Nazi time as the good old days was *Lili Marleen*. All the others have been attempts to earth out the unpleasantness, as opposed to white-washing it. Two East German films have been rather fine: *Jacob The Liar* suggests Nazi brutality and Jewish victimization. I felt a certain authenticity about ghetto life in that film. I wish the second film, *The Fiancée*, were shown more often in every country, but it has never come to America because it was never purchased for international distribution. *The Fiancée* is from 1981, I believe, co-directed by Günter Reisch and Gunther Rücker. It has nothing to do with Jews; it has everything to do with the viciousness of certain Germans and the extraordinary capacity for resistance by certain German prisoners. It's about Communists. Even though I do not share the views of the central characters, this film gave me an extraordinary insight into what it must have been like to fight against the reigning ideology, to put your life on the line for it, to be imprisoned for it and, once imprisoned, to try to give the other prisoners a sense of their own dignity, in an attempt to fight back against the Nazis. It's a great film.

*You indicated in your book that the East European films often deal more effectively in some ways with these themes. Why is that?*

World War Two has been *de rigueur* material in Poland and other countries. After the war almost every film made reflected the devastation experienced by the people of those countries. There were better films made in Europe, in Czechoslovakia and Poland, simply because they were made by people directly touched by the events of World War Two. There's something biographical about them. Moreover, they have access to the places and individuals and experiences— they can shoot in Treblinka, in Auschwitz. Thirdly, East European films are made by a system rather different from ours. You can't make a film unless the censor board approves it, but you do not have the censorship of the box office. Will this film make money? Can we make this film if it doesn't star Maximilian Schell and Sophia Loren? In Eastern Europe, there have been many small-budget films, intended for relatively small audiences.

For example, take the Polish film called *The Passenger*. It was made in 1961 by Andrzej Munk. In the film, a woman who has been an SS Commandant in Auschwitz recollects her experiences. We see two versions. The first version is her attempt at self-justification—she shows how she saved a political prisoner. We know it's all self-serving, because it's shown through her eyes. We never see her, except in a mirror; it's all her own projection, so to speak. In the second part we see her with an objective camera: we see that she's been lying all the time, that she's just as vicious as the next one. The Eastern Europeans use these cinematic techniques that dislocate, that make the viewer cry and remember, and get angry, and walk out feeling that we're not going to let this happen again. In America, we don't do that very often.

*In your book you talk about films, like* Jacob The Liar, *that have comic overtones, some sheer grotesquerie, some quite genuine. Do you think that is a combination that works?*

From the stories I've heard from my parents, their friends and other survivors, one of the things that enabled them to survive was, indeed, a sense of humour—a capacity to transform situations through imagination, through dream, through telling stories, through black humour. I think, however, that this was infinitely more possible in ghettos and in hiding than in concentration camps. I don't mean to suggest that my mother told jokes in Auschwitz, so she survived. Films like *Seven Beauties* are very controversial. I'm always defending that one because everyone is so quick to attack it. *The Great Dictator* and *To Be Or Not To Be*, Lubitsch's film in 1942 with Jack Benny and Carole Lombard as Polish actors evading the Gestapo by putting on a show on stage and off stage as well—these convey something of the Holocaust in the blackness of the humour, in the ironies, the paradoxes, the complexities. Sometimes people survived by assuming identities, by telling tales. Sometimes they survived by improvising, and these films very often give you that sense.

*You also discuss films that you call "beautiful evasions," in which Jews are depicted as absolute perfection, assimilated aristocrats being dragged from their protected lives of privilege and pleasure ineluctably into the Holocaust without fully understanding why. This is dealt with in* The Garden Of The Finzi-Contini. *Does this kind of self-indulgent portrayal of a very small class make you uneasy?*

That's a good word, uneasy, because I think that *The Garden Of The Finzi-Contini* and *Lacombe, Lucien* are beautiful films. They are very well made. They're dramatically powerful. I show them in my classes. But for many of these blond, blue-eyed, high-class, assimilated Jews, their Jewish identity is not just secondary, but really hidden somewhere inside them. They don't feel Jewish. They don't act Jewish, whatever that means.

I become uneasy, because these films might suggest to certain contemporary audiences that most of the Jews who were hounded during the Holocaust were wealthy and blond and assimilated. In fact, the bulk of the Jews who were victims were likely Yiddish-speaking clerks. There were many more impoverished Jews than aristocratic ones. It's a distortion to the extent that we haven't seen many films dealing with the dark-haired, dark-eyed Jews. My own identification with the characters of these films is with their loss in terms of dispossession. They're suddenly stripped of class: they're stripped of their beautiful houses and clothes and possessions. At the end, they're suddenly just normal people being herded off, not because they're Jews. That's a kind of evasion, you have to admit.

*It's interesting that you should be unsettled by that distortion, but not by some other distortions.*

True. Here I'm not talking about why so many films depict Jews as poor and victimized and hardly resisting. That's another problem, which I do raise in my chapter on political resistance. I'm extremely upset by the paltry number of films that deal with the Jewish resistance. For example, *The Wall* was shown on CBS in 1982. It was one of the first examples of a film that showed Jews standing up for themselves as Jews, organizing as Jews, because it was taking place within the Warsaw ghetto. It presented a sorely needed image. Eastern European films, which are wonderful in depicting political resistance—they really show organized action against the Nazis—tend to do so at the expense of Jewish survivors or Jewish prisoners. They, too, tend to show Jews as so concerned about their racial identity and praying and letting God take care of it, that they don't pick up arms. That's a distortion.

One of the problems is that all existing footage of the Holocaust, of ghettos and of concentration camps, was taken with German cameras. If film-makers today want to base their films on reality, they go to archival footage. What do they see? Poor starving faces that elicit sympathy, but very few defiant Jewish faces to elicit respect. How could we have such images? German cameras could not and would not show the faces of people organizing an uprising. The Soviet cameras and the Allied cameras came in only at the point of liberation. People today just don't realize that what we have, while it is real, is only half the picture.

*Are there any Israeli films that speak to the Holocaust?*

There's one very fine documentary called *The 81st Blow.* I was going to include it in my book, but we got short on space and we decided, my editors and I, that fictional films should receive more attention than documentaries. I do not, off-hand, know of any Israeli fiction films. There was one, which was, curiously enough, an Israeli-West German co-production. It was made in the early 1970s, by Aleksander Ford, a Polish-Jewish director, who had to leave Poland when the anti-Semitic purges took place after World War Two. He went to Israel and made this film about Janusz Korczak, who had been an extraordinary figure in the Warsaw ghetto, and who chose to die with his two hundred children from the orphanage. When he was offered his freedom, he chose to go with the children.

It's a fictional reconstruction, and the only Israeli fictional film about the Holocaust that I know. To me, that is perfectly comprehensible. From what I've seen of the Israelis, they are a very forward-looking people. They're very concerned about the present and the future. They're concerned with the past only insofar as it must be used to combat present dangers.

*I wonder if it isn't, perhaps, Elie Wiesel's point that Jews, survivors and non-survivors in a community of Jews, don't feel they can render the Holocaust on film.*

Perhaps in Israeli society they don't feel that they have to. To a great extent, anyone who is living in Israel today understands the legacy of the Holocaust. They know why they're there. They know the price. They know why they don't have grandparents. In a sense, it is not as necessary for an Israeli film-maker to deal with the Holocaust as it is for a German film-maker to deal with the Holocaust. A German film-maker uses cinema to unearth what happened and to face it. The Israelis know what happened and, to some extent, they have faced it.

*Would* The Tin Drum *be perhaps the strongest metaphor, have the greatest impact of modern German film?*

I don't think it's a film about the Holocaust. The novel was not really about the Holocaust either. Perhaps I should have started our conversation by defining the word Holocaust. We're using the term "nuclear holocaust" these days, but it tends to have a small *h*. When it has a big *H* it refers to World War Two and specifically to the destruction of European Jewry. I believe that is the first definition. Secondly, I use the word to include the rise of the Nazi mentality and the post-war legacy. I use it as an umbrella word to refer not only to what happened to the Jews, but also to the question of how it happened within the Nazi mentality, within the French collaborative mentality, within the Eastern European political-resistent mentality. I don't think that the Holocaust means only Jews. I think it means Jews first, and, of course, afterwards it means gypsies, and Communists, and homosexuals, and Germans who resisted the Nazis.

This is the definition that permitted me to include *Sophie's Choice*, *The Tin Drum* and *Our Hitler* in the book. I am going into this because other people, whom I respect, have used the term in a different sense. For them, Holocaust is specifically the Jewish experience in World War Two. This is the sense in which Elie Wiesel uses it, and rightfully so. I guess what I'm doing now is giving you the differences in degree, rather than kind. In fact, when I asked Schlondorff, to what extent *The Tin Drum* was really about the Holocaust, he said, "It's not. Günter Grass was up to something different; I'm up to something different." He admitted that he was trying to deal with a certain Fascist mentality. I suggested my rather outrageous metaphorical reading of the film, in which Jews and midgets were sort of interchangeable. The toy store owner, Sigismund Markus, played by Charles Aznavour, is tiny, you know, like Oskar, and I was wondering if there was some implicit visual equation being made about these people who were diminished and couldn't fight back. He thought that was cute, but it didn't come near what he was up to.

Whether or not it illuminates a lot about the Holocaust, I think it holds up as an indictment of the era, an extremely lush and stylized approach to a terrible period of history.

*If we're talking about that kind of evocation of a period as much as of the Holocaust, does* Cabaret *do a presentable job?*

Absolutely. I was almost surprised, upon seeing *Cabaret* again recently, at how well it illuminated something about the period. Sure it's a great film: it's a wonderful musical, it deserved its Oscars and its box-office success. But you know something? It really works as a dislocating, tension-producing film. You're enjoying yourself in the Kit Kat Klub, watching production numbers, and following the love story of Liza Minnelli and Michael York, but you become increasingly aware of what is happening in the background. Background is becoming foreground until the last shot of the film, that tableau, as the camera pans the distorted faces, the gross visages with the Nazi arm bands predominating. I think the film succeeds in its juxtaposition of musical-production numbers with stories about that era—stories, albeit, about an aristocratic Jew, once again.

*The moment in the film where the young boy sings "The Future Belongs To Me," and the entire audience rises, was such a faithful reflection of German society as a whole. Here they all are, every class, every kind, every person saluting their Führer in advance.*

Absolutely. It's one of the most frightening moments I've ever seen in a film, because the technique is so well done. It begins with a close-up on the face of this angelic boy, creating empathy, identification, and slowly the camera pulls back to reveal the arm band, the other Nazi kids, German society at large. Finally, the moving back of the camera implicates the movie-theatre audience within that frame. I think it makes you realize what you have to guard against, how dangerous it is to be swept up in mass emotion. We all go to movies, and rock concerts, and political rallies, and it's that emotion that is being tapped in the scene.

*Do you feel, on balance, that film is the best way to deal with the phenomenon of the Holocaust?*

That's a tough one. I am not sure. Reading Fania Fenelon's book, *Playing For Time*, made me feel more devastated than seeing it on CBS, even though the film was very well done. Seeing photographs of faces in the Warsaw ghetto or elsewhere sometimes does tell me more than an entire narrative film. Certain poems have captured bits of horror and bits of resistance. I think it's possible to do paintings, too, that convey something. I want to believe that films are capable of communicating something of the experience of the Holocaust, yet I must acknowledge that it might not be the best way these days. Perhaps in fifty years, when film-makers can avoid some clichés and use new developments in technology in a more tension-producing fashion. Perhaps when we have more distance from the events. Frankly, I'm not sure right now.

# Hans Jürgen Syberberg

Hans Jürgen Syberberg was born in Pomerania in 1935, and spent his childhood on his father's estate in the region, which was divided between East Germany and Poland after the Second World War. In 1953 he moved to West Germany, and spent much time travelling about Western Europe before studying literature and art history in Munich.

Between 1956 and 1965 he produced over eighty television shorts and one feature-length documentary before embarking on his own productions. His major work is his trilogy of one hundred years of German-European history: *Ludwig—Requiem for a Virgin King* (1972), *Karl May—In Search of Paradise Lost* (1974), and *Our Hitler—A Film From Germany* (1977), which has gained critical recognition across Europe and North America. His film interview with Richard Wagner's daughter-in-law and friend of Hitler, *The Confessions of Winifred Wagner*, was shown on the American Public Broadcasting System.

Syberberg is an immensely fascinating figure whose words translate into print only with difficulty. Our transatlantic conversation was frequently marred by repetition and misunderstanding. Worse, I had not seen the film *Our Hitler*, so that it was left to Mr. Syberberg, in groping English phrases, to describe its nature, substance and visual impact.

We were both saved by his engaging and tumultuous verbosity which drove all doubt before it. He is, in his opinions, a most courageous fellow.

---

*Mr. Syberberg, the construction of your trilogy, the finale of which is* Our Hitler, *is an immense project. What caused you to embark on such an extraordinary undertaking?*

Actually, when I started to make *Ludwig* in the early 1970s, I did not know that it would continue this way. But in the film there was a sequence of Ludwig's nightmare of Hitler dancing a rhumba—a nightmare of the future. In this nightmare a figure is speaking about the future. At the end of the Ludwig film, I realized that I would like these characters to continue in these next films, as a trilogy. I made *Our Hitler* in 1977, yet I decided to do it in 1972. So you see, it took a lot of time and energy, and it was not easy to get the money for it. As you know, *Our Hitler* is seven hours long, and the money from the BBC and French TV had to be organized.

The problem at that time was to find a special aesthetic, because I knew that I could not do something like the films we are used to. If you compare my work with *Holocaust* from Hollywood, you see the difference. I wanted to get it all, to get into the core of the whole thing. That means no story-telling aesthetic and, of course, no figure like the Hitler we know from newsreels. It is clear that the main strength of a man like Hitler was that he was such a good actor, at least in newsreels. So we could never compete with him or find an actor to play Hitler realistically.

*You once said, "We have to find a new style, a new aesthetic to describe the history of those fifty million dead. It was not only my task to rebuild history, but to go beyond it." I take it you're saying, Mr. Syberberg, that the traditional documentary and narrative-cinema forms simply wouldn't work for a subject of this kind.*

That's right. It's easy to see, looking back; but the first step was to define what had not yet been done. We had to find something different. So our first decision was to use puppets for the main historical characters. You know there's a long tradition of puppetry in German literature and culture: the basis of Goethe's Faust was a puppet play—not one for children like plays today, but one that would have been played in the market for an adult audience. Kleist wrote an essay about puppets, which is very important for German philosophy and aesthetic. So I tried to introduce Hitler and his entourage as puppets. (There is also a Hitler figure who is not a puppet. He comes out of the grave of Richard Wagner, but he is not the Hitler of the newsreels—he is a Hitler who exists only in our fantasy. So he could speak words that we created.)

Then I had to surround these main figures with secondary things, such as Hitler's servant. In this case, this man did exist, but he's not usually considered important enough, in terms of the Holocaust, to appear in films—all those twentieth-of-July films, of the resistance, and so on.

So on one hand I used a Hitler that never existed, and on the other hand I used somebody who really existed but whom historians don't take seriously. I tried to combine elements around the central, important fact. What was important was not Hitler, but the people who voted for him and who are the Hitlers in the end. Because without them, Hitler would not have had any power—he was not a strong character. I think his power came from the people who went with him, or for him, to Stalingrad or wherever.

*Your reply triggers a number of questions. One of them flows from Hitler rising from Wagner's grave. The use of music in · the film is quite overpowering and unusual. Apart from the race of collage and images and techniques, music is a very important aspect in the film. How does it fit with what you were attempting to create?*

I used music partly because music is the heart of German culture. It was used very much in the Nazi period. It was an important cultural tool with the help of Furtwängler and even von Karajan in his early days. But that is not the only reason I used it. Since I was not telling a story it was important to make some kind of montage, because film has its roots in the possibilities of montage. (In earlier times it was a montage of pictures—Eisenstein was a great master of that.) I try to use the soundtrack with a combination of pictures in a special way. One aspect was music, the other possibility, of course, "words," the soundtrack of radio newsreels and so on. In this, of course, music, especially that of Wagner, was very important.

I surrounded the whole seven-hour Hitler film with music: of *Parsifal* at the beginning and at the end, and in the middle, other music, either specially performed by Nazi-party orchestras or other performances of the time. (The recording of *Parsifal*, however, is modern, conducted by Boulez.) When Hitler comes out of the grave of Wagner in the garden of Bayreuth, I used contrasting music from *Rienzi*. Hitler always pointed out that *Rienzi*, one of Wagner's early works, was very important.

*You said earlier, in effect, that Hitler was democratically elected, and therefore Hitler was speaking for all those who put him where he was, rather than demagogically directing them. Isn't it an enormous burden of guilt for the German people collectively? Don't you feel a little benumbed by it, a little reduced by it?*

That was an on-going argument among the German

immigrants in America during the war period. There was Thomas Mann and there was Brecht. I think Brecht was the one who said there are the Nazis, the Hitlers, and then there are the German people. Like Stalin, he said, the Hitlers come and go, but the German people remain. The good Germans go with us—that means with the Communists. Thomas Mann said no, that everyone is guilty, even if he is not a Nazi, for being part of the German community and for coming out of this culture. They should be ashamed, and all are somewhat guilty.

I take the more difficult, latter way. It is a great burden, but it is also something that can be very helpful in later life. Going through a serious illness can strengthen you; you have experienced things that nobody else has known. Maybe when you recover from this sickness, you are wiser than others because you went through it. The problem is that not everyone can or wants to go through it. I am not of the war generation; I was nine years old in May 1945. But I took it on as my part of being German. Maybe in the end it's helpful to know history not only out of books, but from people who are the product of that history.

*In* Our Hitler, *you have the Hitler puppet gloating over the Stalinist purges, the condemnation of Israel in the United Nations, Idi Amin, oppression and torture in South America, Vietnam and Cambodia. There is the suggestion that Hitler lives in these other episodes of human depravity. Do you really think that there is a legitimate analogy? Do you not feel that World War Two and the Holocaust were qualitatively different from some of these barbaric impulses that followed it?*

Since I made the Hitler film five or six years ago, I'm increasingly convinced that we are the heirs of the Hitler period. "Holocaust" is a household word—atomic holocaust. When I made this film six years ago in Israel, I could not have imagined the events of last summer, when even the Israeli opposition condemned the government of its own country by comparing its actions to the Holocaust. Imagine such accusations being made by and against Israelis! It is horrible to say so, but it's on-going. When I made the film maybe it was partly vision, a game of an artist; but today, real events are much more powerful than my fantasy.

*You feel vindicated in what you said in the film.*

Yes, I think reality has very quickly become much more terrible than I could imagine.

*When you dealt with the Holocaust in the film, you distanced yourself. While Himmler was having a massage, the voice-over was describing the liquidation of the Russian Jews. You avoided, as Susan Sontag says in her review, that "frontal assault on the senses," which pictures of the camps evoke. She said, "To stimulate atrocities convincingly is to risk making the audience passive, reinforcing witless stereotypes, confirming distance, and creating meretritious fascination." In other words, trivializing the event by dealing with it head on. Are you still of that opinion?*

I think very often we fail when we try to describe cruelties that we know took place. We speak very easily about the times being dangerous. Maybe we speak about the guilt of our parents, especially in Germany, and about what can happen; but mostly we look in the wrong direction. We look into the past, and we look at trivial events. The only reason to deal with history—not as an historian but as an artist and as an active, responsible man—is to find the corruption in our time. Of course, there's no Hitler today, but the evil is always there, hidden in other things. It is our responsibility to find the evil sources.

The only reason to deal with history in the arts is to make it come alive for our time and relate to our problems. Otherwise it's a museum piece. You must always get to the point at which it hurts. If you are not hurt, if it is not provocative, then you have failed. You always have to push a little bit farther—not in a cheap way, because it is good business or entertainment; but we must find the danger point. Things portrayed in *Our Hitler* five or six years ago have actually happened since then. When I look back on this film, I'm always astonished and horrified to find how far I went into the reality of our time.

*Why did you avoid using available concentration-camp film? A lot of it is German footage taken by German photographers because Hitler was fascinated by film. Why did you deal only indirectly, elliptically, by voice-over, with the reality of the camps?*

We have lots of footage, lots of newsreels; every now and then new ones are found. But until now no one had any document to prove that Hitler himself decreed the killing of the Jews, so film did not force anyone to be convinced. But I discovered these recordings of Himmler speaking—his own voice talking about killing the Jews and how difficult it is for his people, but it has to be done, and so on and so on. This is a document that nobody can ignore. It proves that commands really came out of the mouth of this man. So I take the document, the soundtrack of Himmler speaking of the killing of the Jews in the east, and combine it with pictures of Himmler's massage and his visions. I bring this important document alive much more than any newsreels of that time do. The technique of a voice document with a new picture has been used very often since, in different ways, so obviously people got the message. I think the technique is used to force belief—it seems more believable than any newsreel we know. People often speak about newsreels as if they don't believe them. But you have to believe the voice of Himmler, simply because it's really his voice—nobody ever denied that it was the voice of Himmler. And of course in combination with the pictures it is more horrible than I had imagined. But of course it must be done very precisely, just as much as is bearable. If you go farther, the viewer shuts his ears and eyes, and it doesn't work.

*You are a man utterly devoted to film. You've called it the music of the future, the continuation of life, the total work of art of our age. You even once extravagantly said, "He who has film has life." Do you truly feel that if important events are to be communicated to the world at large, film is the medium through which the communication should proceed?*

Yes, but I think it works slowly. Just yesterday evening, we had a discussion about the forged Hitler diaries. Someone compared *Our Hitler* to the *Holocaust* series from Hollywood. *Holocaust* would have no influence on the people after one or two years. People were very easily influenced at the moment, maybe for days, maybe weeks, but then it was gone. But a film like *Our Hitler* works very slowly. You cannot say that after one week, after one month, maybe after one year, it changes the minds of millions of people; but I think it slowly brings justice to history, like all art does. I think that's very important. For instance, American politicians after the war had to work with the Nazis because they wanted information from them about Russia. Even Israelis worked with some Germans, because they needed their help against *present* enemies. Politics is very dirty. It has to be dirty because that is life. But art can escape the realities of every-day politics. Art can bring honour to a country or era, and it can unite countries, but of course it does not alter history. Art has to be very moral, because it works slowly over generations. That's the problem. Wagner can create *Parsifal* and be anti-Semitic. Years after his death, this anti-Semitism can become the Holocaust. Art can be used by Hitler as well as by Einstein.

*Do you think that, ultimately, film is more persuasive than literature in conveying these paradoxes?*

Yes, I think film is the art of this century. Film has more possibilities than books, than theatre or music in concert halls. They are marvellous aspects of our being, but they are only part. I think film has possibilities to become what we call in German "*Gesamtkünstwerk.*" It has something of the power that the cathedrals had in the Middle Ages. Film can use pictures and soundtracks and words and lift the whole being of an audience into a new world of self-understanding. That's something new, that our age has created.

*You use your daughter in the film. Why and how?*

I think that is related to the puppet idea. There is a certain innocence in a child. We can use that quality to create something between a puppet and an actor. If one uses not only a child but one's own child, then, of course, you are taking the idea to the limit, you begin to create art.

In *Our Hitler*, my daughter is the essence of somebody wandering through the story. It's all done for her, really. She is the only judge, the ideal audience—more than an audience. During the course of the film, she ages five years. She became something between a child and a grown-up, but still an innocent. I needed this innocence to complete the pattern of the film more than I needed a child. So her growing older created good continuity.

*When you completed the film, you initially refused to let it be shown in Germany. I understand that you have a long-standing difference of opinion with German film critics over the way in which they deal with your work. To what extent did you not get along with them, or appreciate the criticism, and to what extent were you influenced by the way Germans might react to a film of this kind?*

I think it was not a discussion at all, but a confrontation—not about the subject, but about aesthetics. They didn't like the film; they didn't agree with the way it was made. They preferred *Holocaust* from Hollywood, because it comes from America, and America is master of our art and thinking—we are only a colony. But they also hated or avoided my aesthetic innovation and they criticized my "aestheticizing" politics. But after a while they stopped.

There is not one German critical analysis of *Our Hitler* that is even one page long, let alone anything comparable to, say, Susan Sontag's long analysis. But of course, we know what they think, and the aggressiveness of the criticism is very painful for me. I also realize it would be dangerous to keep the audience away, because I think they have to go through the experience; otherwise they will never, for instance, really enjoy Wagner again. He has to be freed through this painful work.

But it's not only a problem with the film critics. The behaviour of all the others, too, is a problem. You know, I made a film that deals a lot with music, and I was criticized by the music people. Then I wrote books, and there was opposition from the literary critics in the papers. Then I had an exhibition in Zurich, and the art critics rejected what I had done. My problem is being first  I put my finger in the wound.

*The German critics like something as tawdry and unrepresentative and dishonest as* Holocaust, *yet they don't like the aesthetics of* Our Hitler *because it raises all the questions provocatively. That says something, does it not, about the way in which the German people are dealing with 1933 to 1945?*

That's exactly the problem. Very often it is said that some Germans are still dangerous because they are neo-Nazis, but these poor creatures are not important. Others ignore the issue by saying that there is now a new Germany. Now the western world—even the eastern world—needs the German army and needs to trade with Germany. Sometimes they punish them a little to get better business deals, but that is not the issue. The problem is much deeper and no one wants to face it. For instance, three times they refused to let me make new films—it's censorship. It's not only a man here who hates Syberberg or three critics there who don't like my films. No. There are all sorts of commissions, independent commissions from outside Germany. You cannot say that all these people are my enemies. No, there is something in the air. After the Hitler films there was no money for another film. I tried to raise money, as all my colleagues do, for *Parsifal,* and everyone said no. After *Parsifal* I needed money for a new film; again they said no. These decisions are made by different independent organizations, or by the government. They just don't want to have to deal with more of my work. But on the other hand, of course, there is a lot of interest in this country. It's very difficult to let people know about *Our Hitler* or *Parsifal* without the help of the media. But if they come, you often have very good discussions.

*When* Our Hitler *was eventually shown, what was the response? Did you get hate letters? Did you get phone calls that were abusive and unfriendly?*

No, mostly not. When I got personal reactions, they were marvellous ones: long letters, very often from young people, even younger than I am, the post-war generation, speaking about their parents. When I was insulted or hurt, it was by the media. Bashing Syberberg is good for the career of a critic. That's the problem.

When I compare the reception of the films in other countries—Italy, France, England, America, Spain or Portugal—it's like being another person in another life. I do have a certain success even in Germany. But it is a covert one. Enemies pat me on the back when they are drunk, or in secret, but they don't do it officially.

# Elie Wiesel

Elie Wiesel was born in 1928 in Sighet, in the Romanian province of Transylvania. In 1944 he was deported and spent two years in Birkenau, Auschwitz, Monowitz and Buchenwald. After the war he went to France, studied at the Sorbonne and worked as a journalist. Since 1956 he has lived in New York, where, until 1976, he was Distinguished Professor of Judaic Studies at City College, City University of New York. At present he is Andrew W. Mellon Professor in the Humanities at Boston University. Wiesel has received twenty-three honorary doctorates and countless awards and citations for his work, including the *Prix Bourdin de l'Academie Française*, the *Prix Medicis*, the *Bourse Goncourt*, and the International Literary Prize for Peace from the Royal Academy of Belgium.

He has published over twenty novels, plays, collections of essays, memoirs, short stories and a cantata, as well as numerous articles for newspapers and journals. Wiesel and his work are the subject of twelve book-length studies.

Elie Wiesel is married and has a son, Elisha.

My encounter with Elie Wiesel took place on a crowded sofa in the hospitably cluttered library of his New York home. The interview was influenced by our cheek-by-jowl proximity— that is to say, there was an intimacy and intensity which, I feel sure, would not have occurred in a recording studio. I was anxious. The media have always presented Wiesel—or so it seemed to me—as "the survivor" incarnate. I was ready to respect him, but not necessarily to like him. I was wrong. He has a charismatic, almost biblical presence, and though the eyes are forever sad, and the voice forever tinged with pain, there is a warmth and a humanity that completely embrace the listener. I found myself hanging on every word, much as a son, at certain crucial moments in life, seeks response and explanation from a father. I felt as though I received it.

*Why do you think there has been such a burst of literature and film dealing with the Holocaust in the last two or three years?*

Some reasons are superficial, others are profound. Superficially, it is the commercial motivation. What sells is what is being offered. People want to know, and people want to know superficial things. The easier it is to understand, the easier to absorb the event, the better it is for them. The profound reason is that the subject has been suppressed for so many years that now it is bursting forth. Therefore, you have it in all the various forms of art: movies, television, literature, poetry, history. Which is good, by the way; I applaud it, if it is being done with respect and sensitivity.

*You say that the subject has been repressed all these years. Are the reasons for that endemic to the survivor, or are they a little sinister or conspiratorial?*

Not conspiratorial, no. People did not want to know. People were afraid to know. They all felt threatened, guilty, accused, indicted. So, on one hand, the survivors did not speak because they knew they would not be understood. They still think so, as I do. On the other hand, they also knew that the tale had to be told. Hence the difficulty, the obstacle. How are we to say the things that must be said and yet we know cannot be said? As a result, there was a certain silence. For many, many years, you could not publish a book on the subject. My first book, *Night*, went from publisher to publisher in the United States, and all the major publishers refused it.

The Holocaust defied words, language, imagination, knowledge. For many years we believed this, we still believe it, except now we accept it less. Now we say that if people listen to at least a fragment of the story, it is enough. But in the beginning, there was so much to tell, and the recurring phrase on our lips was: he wouldn't understand. In 1945 to 1947, people would ask what happened. And all of us would simply say, we cannot tell—you wouldn't understand. True. Nobody could understand the misery, the fear, the anguish, the pain, the hunger, the humiliation, the infinite humiliation of a person who was to be the absolute victim. How did I survive one day, one night? How did I see and remain sane, if I remained sane? How was it possible to endure so many nightmares and such despair? To this day, I do not understand. Well, I don't understand many things: the complicity of the spectators, the indulgence of the bystanders, the evil of the killers, the suffering of the victims, the silence of God—I don't understand anything. How can you explain, how can you express what you do not understand?

*Do you still hold to the view that non-survivors should not try to capture the events?*

I never said that. Everybody has the right to deal with the subject—novelists and poets and painters and musicians—if it is in the direction of our anguish, and does not disarm it. I think John Hersey wrote a great novel, *The Wall*. Nelly Sachs was never in a camp, yet she wrote poetry about that experience. Paul Célan was never in Auschwitz and yet his poems are about that experience. If a novelist is ready to face the darkness, if a poet is ready to face that anguish honestly, and not for cheap, easy reasons, anyone can deal with the subject.

*One has the sense in many things you've written that you doubt that the Holocaust is within the grasp of fiction.*

Unfortunately, part of our tragedy is that it will not be known. Even if all of us who were there and who were not there did nothing else for our entire lives but write about it, still the story would not be told. The moment it is said, it isn't; the moment it is offered, it is withdrawn. The only language may be a mystical language, and that language is a language shrouded in silence. Will it ever be told? I have probably read all the books that have come out on the subject. I am fascinated by these books. I always hope I will discover something else, something more, so I read history, I read philosophy, I read documents, I read fiction, everything. I do not know more, I know less.

*What do you feel about a novel like* Sophie's Choice?

I would not single out any novel, because I know Styron. I have met him a few times, and I respect his craft; I respect his literary skill, and in a way I applaud his effort. Personally, of course, I must say, as I have written in the *Times,* that I do not recognize myself in films such as *Sophie's Choice,* but that may be my fault, not his. Nobody should fault him for his intention to write a novel like *Sophie's Choice.* Why shouldn't he? He is a writer who lives in his time, and he wants to deal with contemporary issues, and what issue is greater or more urgent than that one? Now, whether it succeded as a novel, maybe the answer is yes. But because he succeeded, in a way he may have failed. Because a novel about Auschwitz is either not a novel or it is not about Auschwitz.

*The terms are incompatible?*

They are unfortunately incompatible. That is the nature and the substance of that tragedy: art and Auschwitz somehow do not go together. *Sophie's Choice* is not about the Holocaust. It is not the Holocaust that is there. Mine is probably a minority voice. I am the only one who said it or will say it. But I feel almost duty-bound. That is why I wrote a piece in The *New York Times* about the whole phenomenon, not about *Sophie's Choice* as such. But from time to time we must simply say that, humbly, in an atmosphere of modesty. That is all we can do, simply say: no, it is not what we had hoped it to be.

*Styron and others expand the meaning of the word Holocaust to incorporate something more than the annihilation of six million Jews. They resist the proposition that it should be appropriated as a Jewish phenomenon.*

Oh, I know they do that, I know they say that. It is too bad, because they put us in a situation I don't like. I do not like to seem to be denigrating or diminishing other peoples' suffering. It so happens I was among the first, if not the first, to use the term Holocaust to describe this tragedy, and I am sorry; I should not have done that; I regret it. There is no word, really. I remember having chosen the word because of its mystical and its religious connotations. I wanted to show that the event was more than a political event, than a simple war, more than a pogrom. It was something else—it was beyond. But now I am embarrassed to use the word, because it has become so cheap and so diluted.

Now, let us be honest, intellectually and morally and humanly honest. True, there were other people who suffered then, but not the same way. Only the Jewish people were designated for total murder. Only the Jew was guilty simply because he was a Jew. In other words, we Jews were not condemned to death because we were human beings, but because we were Jews. Which means that, for the first time in history, "being" became a crime. And that was true for only the Jew and the Jewish victim, and nobody else. That does not mean others did not suffer. There were many members of the resistance who were shot; there were many gypsies who were killed; there were many civilians who were dragged to the concentration camps, and they, too, were killed. But somehow it is not the same thing. Why should we now facilitate Hitler's plan posthumously? He wanted to wipe out the Jewish memory. If we did what others now want us to do, we would be diluting our memory in such a way that it would disappear. Soon they will speak about, let us say, eight million, nine million, eleven million. We can make a game of numbers, and in fifty years they will speak of thirty million civilians, and then they will simply say there was a war, and the whole tragedy will be reduced to a phrase: "man's inhumanity to man." Well, I think it would be a betrayal of the victims. Those people died only because they were Jews, and that is why we must remember them as such. That does not mean we exclude others. That means that we include others, but differently.

*Does that mean that the only authentic accounts can come from the pens and the recollections of the survivors?*

Authentic, yes. Obviously only the witnesses can bear testimony. But the survivors are not the only group. I will go further: the authentic documents come from the dead. We find chronicles, chronicles written by the Sondercommandos, the commanders who were doing the burning of the corpses. A book just appeared in France, which I have prefaced, called *Voix dans la nuit, Voices in the Night,* chronicles found literally under the ashes in Birkenau, written by Sondercommandos. While they were burning their families, their communities, they managed to keep diaries. I can tell you, with all the strength and the faith that I have, that no book equals theirs. So the real witnesses are the dead and the authentic accounts come from the dead.

*But many would presumably argue that, given the state of universal ignorance, on the one hand, and resistance to this kind of truth, on the other, it's necessary to have contemporary novels and films, even if they trivialize, in order to give the world a glimmer of what took place.*

You have mentioned the word *argue.* I do not really want to participate in that argument. I do not like controversy on the subject, and I rarely debate it. To me, to some of us, it is beyond argument, or beyond dispute or discussion. If our words are being received, it is all right. What else can we do? I gave up hope long ago of being able, without testimony, to change the world. Now I think we are more modest; we are simply trying to tell the tale as purely, as soberly, as we can. You say that more people would know. True. But if the choice is between a trivialization of the event and nothing, I prefer nothing. If people know nothing, then one day they will know, but if they know this trivialized, cheapened, or distorted version then surely they will remember the distorted, trivialized view, and ultimately they falsify memory.

*Annette Insdorf might respond by saying that even if the* Holocaust *film on television was a travesty in its portrayal, and in its submission to commercial interests, nonetheless it unleashed in post-war Germany and in parts of the United States a flood of writing and film-making that was truer to the art, truer to the episode of history, and that therefore makes it legitimate.*

I do not agree. I think that the film did more harm than good, because it created the precedent that vulgarity is possible. Once you open the floodgates of vulgarity, who will stop it? No: remember, I have seen the series and I responded to it in the *New York Times.* The things they showed, the stupidities they accumulated, for example, having a woman bring her photographs and music sheets into Birkenau, having her husband come and be with her and love her! They did not know that there was a men's camp and a women's camp, that it was impossible to leave one for the other without being shot. If that was Birkenau, I do not want it to be remembered as such. I want the truth to be remembered. In that case, speaking about films, I would take *Night and Fog*, where they simply showed the empty barracks, and that would carry more power and more truth into the future than these trivialized, spectacular extravaganzas.

*When I watched* Night and Fog, *I felt that I had experienced an emotional catharsis. It was documentary rather than fiction, and it seemed to me absolutely legitimate.*

Absolutely. It is a rare combination of poetry and document and photography. Try to remember, and you will see that the word "Jew" was not even mentioned. Usually, I would resent it; in this case I do not, because it is authentic. When I saw *Night and Fog*, I, too, was overwhelmed by its dark truth. There is another movie called *The 81st Blow*, made in Israel, which is also very powerful. I do not think that the tale cannot be told, but I don't think the tale in its totality will ever be told. I am not even sure that it should be told. Maybe we are not capable of absorbing so much. There is a certain knowledge that one should not explore, because one's sanity is in jeopardy. Maybe sometimes in history winds of madness blow in the world. The Crusades were madness, total madness.

*I felt that* Sophie's Choice *was a violation of everything that had occurred. But people like Styron and his confrères would say, "It's my tragedy, too. I am part of the human condition. I cannot be excluded and however much I may convey it in a fashion that is groping rather than utterly authentic, I am making a contribution to humanity, because I am focussing on humanness."*

There is a difference between the series that we mentioned earlier, *Holocaust*, and *Sophie's Choice*. *Sophie's Choice* did not pretend to be a documentary. The other one did, and therefore we had to protest with greater vigour. I did not protest *Sophie's Choice*. I did not say that Styron was wrong. I did not say that he did anything bad. I simply said that I did not recognize myself in it, that is all.

*What happens when there are no survivors left?*

That is, of course, the obsession that is haunting us. Somewhere in one of my novels I have tried to imagine that last survivor. I do not want to be that survivor. I am afraid of that survivor, of his vision. I'm afraid of the madness that would invade him, weigh upon him, to have so much knowledge and to know that, with him, all this knowledge will go down, will go out. I do not know what will happen, but am terribly pessimistic with regard to the future of humanity.

*The last chapter of* A Jew Today *is quintessential in its pessimism not only for the end of the survivors, but also for those who did not respond to the Holocaust itself and, indeed, have been self-centred in the aftermath. Are you driven to these despairs?*

No. I do whatever I can to fight them. That is why I write so many books about so many other subjects. I write about ecstasy and fervour and joy and happiness in the seventeenth century, or in Biblical times, the Talmudic era. I try to find reasons to be hopeful. It is not easy, not in the present, and yet—that is my favourite expression, "and yet"—there is despair, and yet, on the other hand, there is joy, and yet. Nothing is complete, nothing is whole. In a strange way I believe that, due to our despair, hope is possible, if we face our despair honestly. We must try to go to the end of things to see what has been done to history and the human condition by the fact that a people have been massacred. If we do that, then we may save the world. Paradoxically, out of this despair an awesome hope can be born. If we forget, there is no doubt in my mind that one day there will be a fire that will engulf the planet, and that fire will reflect the fires that once upon a time dominated our days and our nights.

The night had now set in. The snow had ceased to fall. We walked for several more hours before arriving.

We did not notice the camp until we were just in front of the gate.

Some Kapos rapidly installed us in the barracks. We pushed and jostled one another as if this were the supreme refuge, the gateway to life. We walked over pain-racked bodies. We trod on wounded faces. No cries. A few groans. My father and I were ourselves thrown to the ground by this rolling tide. Beneath our feet someone let out a rattling cry:

"You're crushing me . . . mercy!"

A voice that was not unknown to me.

"You're crushing me . . . mercy! mercy!"

The same faint voice, the same rattle, heard somewhere before. That voice had spoken to me one day. Where? When? Years ago? No, it could only have been at the camp.

"Mercy!"

I felt that I was crushing him. I was stopping his breath. I wanted to get up. I struggled to disengage myself, so that he could breathe. But I was crushed myself beneath the weight of other bodies. I could hardly breathe. I dug my nails into unknown faces. I was biting all around me, in order to get air. No one cried out.

Suddenly I remembered. Juliek! The boy from Warsaw who played the violin in the band at Buna. . . .

"Juliek, is it you?"

"Eliezer . . . the twenty-five strokes of the whip. Yes . . . I remember."

He was silent. A long moment elapsed.

"Juliek! Can you hear me, Juliek?"

"Yes . . . ," he said, in a feeble voice. "What do you want?"

He was not dead.

"How do you feel, Juliek?" I asked, less to know the

answer than to hear that he could speak, that he was alive.

"All right, Eliezer.... I'm getting on all right ... hardly any air ... worn out. My feet are swollen. It's good to rest, but my violin...."

I thought he had gone out of his mind. What use was the violin here?

"What, your violin?"

He gasped.

"I'm afraid ... I'm afraid ... that they'll break my violin. ... I've brought it with me."

I could not answer him. Someone was lying full length on top of me, covering my face. I was unable to breathe, through either mouth or nose. Sweat beaded my brow, ran down my spine. This was the end—the end of the road. A silent death, suffocation. No way of crying out, of calling for help.

I tried to get rid of my invisible assassin. My whole will to live was centered in my nails. I scratched. I battled for a mouthful of air. I tore at decaying flesh which did not respond. I could not free myself from this mass weighing down my chest. Was it a dead man I was struggling against? Who knows?

I shall never know. All I can say is that I won. I succeeded in digging a hole through this wall of dying people, a little hole through which I could drink in a small quantity of air.

"Father, how are you?" I asked, as soon as I could utter a word.

I knew he could not be far from me.

"Well!" answered a distant voice, which seemed to come from another world. I tried to sleep.

He tried to sleep. Was he right or wrong? Could one sleep here? Was it not dangerous to allow your vigilance to fail, even for a moment, when at any minute death could pounce upon you?

I was thinking of this when I heard the sound of a violin. The sound of a violin, in this dark shed, where the dead were heaped on the living. What madman could be playing the violin here, at the brink of his own grave? Or was it really an hallucination?

It must have been Juliek.

He played a fragment from Beethoven's concerto. I had never heard sounds so pure. In such a silence.

How had he managed to free himself? To draw his body from under mine without my being aware of it? It was pitch dark. I could hear only the violin, and it was as though Juliek's soul were the bow. He was playing his life. The whole of his life was gliding on the strings—his lost hopes, his charred past, his extinguished future. He played as he would never play again.

I shall never forget Juliek. How could I forget that concert, given to an audience of dying and dead men! To this day, whenever I hear Beethoven played my eyes close and out of the dark rises the sad, pale face of my Polish friend, as he said farewell on his violin to an audience of dying men.

I do not know for how long he played. I was overcome by sleep. When I awoke, in the daylight, I could see Juliek, opposite me, slumped over, dead. Near him lay his violin, smashed, trampled, a strange overwhelming little corpse.

*One of the people who writes superbly, I think, on all of this, in fictional form, is Aharon Appelfeld. He never deals with it directly; he deals tangentially, but with a kind of visceral truth. If one is to approach the Holocaust in fiction, would you consider that to be a more faithful way?*

That is the only way. I have written only one book about that period, a slim, very short volume of autobiographical memoirs. Even there, of course, I tried to write in as lean and austere a way as possible. One word had to consider a hundred, and one face had to hide a hundred.

*And in a sense, Appelfeld does exactly the same thing. His prose is very spare, very elliptical in some ways, always coming around his subject.*

*Jurek Becker was surprisingly uncharitable in his view of many survivors. He talked, in the way no others have talked, about turning on the tear ducts, about pressing the button to get the necessary emotional involvement. He, therefore, found the literature and the approach suspect. Is that just the dismissal of the uninformed?*

No, I think it is unkind and ungracious and unwarranted. Personally, I am also against sentimentality in literature or in life. I do not like to see people showing their wounds or crying or making other people cry. But in this case it is really unfair. These survivors have waited for thirty years to speak, because they did not want other people to cry. Even today, I don't want people to cry. Nobody wants people to cry.

*Are survivors feeling more free to write and to speak about the event?*

I think so. I now get many manuscripts and I encourage them. I would like every survivor to write his or her story, for the sake of history. There is always something new.

*How do other survivors feel about the attempt to deal with the Holocaust in a way that is not true to their experience, but in a way that attempts to educate the rest of the world?*

I do not know. It must be a combination of gratitude and dismay. Gratitude that at last someone tries. And dismay, because those who try think they succeed. If a novelist had said, "I tried this and it hurts and I know I failed," I would like that novelist. But most of them say, "See, I tried, it worked." Then something is wrong about it.

*You cannot then imagine any novelist who was separate from the event capturing it in a way that would reflect the true horror?*

True? What does *true* mean? One sentence written by a poet may express that truth more than a hundred novels. If it is historic truth that we talk about, then it is one thing. If it is philosophical truth, that is another. If it is metaphysical truth, it is still another. And we do not really know what we are seeking there. We try to understand: that was the obsession that we all had, we wanted to understand. There is a man called Yankel Wiernik; he was a carpenter and he was the first to escape from Treblinka to write about it. Mind you, he published his book in 1944. He tells of his arrival in Treblinka and of working together with the Sondercommandos there. He saw the corpses being burned and he had only one question in his mind: "What is the meaning of all that?" Well, that is what I was asking myself when I arrived as a child in Birkenau. "What is the meaning of all that?" I still do not know what the meaning of all that was. I still don't. I am afraid I will never know. I have not found the meaning in those novels. But, again, that should not be held against them, that is not their purpose. Their purpose is to tell a story, and they tell a story—with more or less eroticism, it doesn't matter.

*There's more than a touch of sarcasm when you say, "more or less eroticism."*

Today you cannot write a best-selling novel without that. And again, if you accept the theory that it must be read by as many people as possible, then you have to have a little bit of suspense, a little bit of sex, a very beautiful woman, a very strong or weak man. That is the way to write a novel that people want to read. I am not sure I would like to do that. I do not think I would be able to do it, but that has not been my preoccupation. I do not think that I am here, that I survived, to write that kind of novel.

*So, fundamentally, while you wouldn't begrudge for a moment the novelist's quest for his or her version of truth, at the point at which the trivialization offends, then you would call a halt.*

If it pretended to be the truth, or to be a documentary, I would say, no, that was not the truth. But if it's fiction, I would simply say, "Look, it's fiction, but there is something to which I must personally take exception. I do not think you have represented what we felt, what we lived, or what we died."

*Help me—as a Jew, I understand completely what you're
saying. I know that unless I read your works and those of
other survivors, I can never grasp what occurred. And I know
that others who attempt to convey it are doing it an ultimate
violation. On the other hand, I see the State of Israel
surrounded by predatory, hostile states. I see anti-Semitism
throughout the world. I see the possibility that something
horrific can occur again. I therefore want the Holocaust to be
sufficiently strong in people's minds that decent human beings
this time will intervene, that the entire world won't lapse into
apathy. How does that happen unless some good writers try,
in their own tentative way, to come as close as they can to
what occurred?*

First of all, I am not here to resolve conflicts. You think I
don't have conflicts? You think I don't have tensions and
obstacles? I have more than you can imagine, probably more
than I can imagine. I don't know. I must tell you the truth: I
don't know. I know it is impossible to do and yet I must do it. I
said earlier that I do not think I survived to write certain
books in a certain way. I think that since I survived, by
accident, I have to do something with my life; that is what we
all feel. Therefore, every minute must be justified. I know
when I write, or when I teach, the background is always there.
And whatever I do, and whatever I say, is measured against
that background. I know I have to tell a certain truth in a
certain way and not go down to a certain level, or I will betray
myself. I would turn my whole life into a farce.

You think I have truth? I do not. You think I have an
answer? I do not. All I can ask is for humility. Humility in the
face of so many deaths, of so much fear, of so many tears. In
my mind I always see the processions of children walking,
walking. With these processions in front of you, you don't
play with words, not even with ideas, or sentiments. If I had to
use that event, I would rather be quiet. Not even for Israel. I

would do anything I could to help the Jewish people—to help any people—to help Israel, but I would not use the Holocaust. That is something that should be sacred, not touched.

*Some have changed their minds. In 1967 George Steiner was writing of silence and in 1980 he was writing a novel. He was engulfed, I gather, by the realization that the silence just wasn't good enough. That the world had to know.*

I, too, kept silent for ten years. Then I felt that it was not enough. But what I have tried to do is not to replace silence with words, but to add silence to the words, to surround words with silence. If I cannot communicate a silence within my words, I hope I would know when to stop. I would not say anything.

*Your friend Appelfeld talks a lot about Kafka and his premonitions of what was to come. Do you share that view of Kafka?*

He was, of course, seminal in my life, too. There is a pre-Kafka and a post-Kafka existence in my life. I doubt he had visions. Nobody could imagine what happened. I cannot even imagine it now. Often, I wonder, have I seen what I remember? Have I been there? This is the problem of literary creation nowadays. Once upon a time, imagination preceded reality; now it goes behind reality, and somewhere it is lost. So, did Kafka imagine Auschwitz? No human being could imagine Auschwitz. I don't even think that God could. And yet Kafka was probably, in his fear, in his anguish, in his despair, the one who came closest to the feelings that we now have, the feeling of being the messenger who is trying desperately to deliver the message, and there is no one to receive it.

Remember, Kafka wanted to burn his writings. Why? Nobody really knows. Perhaps he, too, was afraid of the impact they might have on people, just as we are afraid of the effect that our writings may have or should have on people. He wanted to burn them, but luckily, his friend Max Brod saved them. But I always think of a Hasidic master who was actually Franz Kafka's forerunner. He was a great Hasidic story-teller, the greatest of them all, Rabbi Nachman of Bratzlav. He, too, told very fine stories about absurdity and exile. And he, too, ordered his writings to be burned; but his writings *were* burned.

*Do you permit yourself to see the movies that deal with Holocaust themes, to read the books, like* The White Hotel, *which allegedly encompass the event?*

Oh, I read all the books. I only see movies when I have to. But I am not good at images. I do not watch television or movies that often.

*When you read a book like* The White Hotel, *what runs through your mind?*

I would not pass judgement on the book, any more than on *Sophie's Choice*. I feel that D.M. Thomas had the right to write *The White Hotel*. He wanted to write on that subject. It is absolutely his prerogative to do so.

*Do you exercise no literary or cultural criticism when you read a book like* The White Hotel?

I do, but, you know, I am so prejudiced, I am so biased, I admit it: I want the truth, and I know I cannot find it. So I feel sad at times. But also, at the same time, here and there, there is a page in this novel or another novel, where the writer maybe unwillingly says something that surprises me. That page, I am sure, has been written in humility, and therefore it is a good experience. But I know that I could not be an objective reviewer, and therefore I would not review. In general I only review in praise. I have probably written two articles that were negative, and neither of them was about books. One was about a television series, and one was a little bit negative about the film *Sophie's Choice.*

*D.M. Thomas invokes Babi Yar. He said that because the event cannot be encompassed by a novelist he went to the words of the survivor in order to give it legitimacy.*

Therefore, I think he has taken a lot from Kuznetsov. I went twice to Babi Yar. What came to my mind was Jeremiah. Often it is the prophet who has the best words for our experiences. Jeremiah spoke of the ground shaking. I heard from eye-witnesses that, during the days between the Jewish New Year and Yom Kippur, when they killed some eighty thousand Jews, ten thousand a day, and threw them in the mass graves, some of them alive, the ground would not stop shaking for weeks and weeks, and I felt Jeremiah's words. Jeremiah speaks about a kind of air desert, the desert in space. I never understood it until I remembered that there were no birds flying over Auschwitz. So it is not the novelist that helps, it is the prophet that tries to help.

*You have a touch of the Old Testament in some of your writings, which I'm sure you are aware of.*

Oh, I am not aware of it, but if you say so, I am grateful to you. I am a passionate student of scripture, of the prophets, of Talmud. I study every day. And I mean it, every day I study, and I learn and I learn and I learn. Will I be able to communicate what I have absorbed? I hope so.

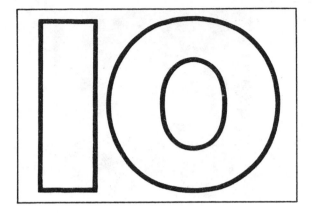

# William Styron

©STATHIS ORPHANOS

William Styron was born in Newport News, Virginia in 1925, and was educated at Duke University. He served with the United States Marine Corps during the Second World War and the Korean War.

He is an essayist, playwright and reviewer, and has served as advisory editor to the *Paris Review* and on the editorial board of *The American Scholar*. His first novel, *Lie Down in Darkness* (1951) was awarded the Prix de Rome of the American Academy of Arts and Letters. *The Confessions of Nat Turner* (1967) received the Pulitzer Prize. His other writings include *Set This House on Fire* (1960) and the play, *In the Clap Shack* (1973). *Sophie's Choice* was published in 1979. His most recent major work is *This Quiet Dust* (1982), a collection of essays, meditations and reviews.

Styron is married and has three children. He lives in Roxbury, Connecticut.

When Styron and I shook hands, his first words were, "I'm told you're a socialist." "Yes," said I. "So am I," he responded. And from that moment on, the interview proceeded with preternatural ease.

Even though Styron has experienced stunning artistic success, there's not a hint of egotism. Every subject was met forthrightly, with no affected, weighty musings. Styron is neither dogmatic nor equivocal—just open and direct. He gave several years of his life to *Sophie's Choice*; it reflects his deepest convictions.

---

Sophie's Choice *was an astonishing and overwhelming success in every sense. How do you account for that?*

I'm not really sure. I think certain books seem to coincide with the *Zeitgeist*, with the spirit of the time. And I think that, at the simplest level, *Sophie's Choice* coincided with a deep and troubled interest in the Nazi period and the Holocaust. In certain ways, ever since World War Two, we have been thinking about the Nazis and the camps and the Holocaust in general, but I think it came to a crescendo in the late 1970s, when my book was published. The book appeared, after all, only a year after that rather sensational and not terribly good television programme, *Holocaust*. In the years preceding the late 1970s there just was not enough general consciousness of what had gone on. Finally the accretion of fact, and the sense of the horror, just grew and grew.

*Is that what happened to you as a novelist? Is that what propelled you?*

I have been interested in the subject ever since the years right after World War Two, when I was in college. The subject fascinated me even then. Although there was not much literature on it then, that changed as time passed. But even then, there was a book, a fascinating book called *Five Chimneys*, by a woman victim of Auschwitz, a survivor who had been a doctor. It is not a terribly literary book but it is a very skilful and graphic description of Auschwitz. I had it in the back of my mind through the period from World War Two until the mid-seventies, when I began to write *Sophie's Choice*.

Having no more tears to shed for the moment, Sophie slowly composed herself. "Thank you, you were kind," she said to me softly, in the stuffed-head-cold tones of one who has wept copiously and long. She stretched out her hand and pressed into my own the handkerchief, a soggy wad. As she did so I saw for the first time the number tattooed on the suntanned, lightly freckled skin of her forearm—a purple number of at least five digits, too small to read in this light but graven, I could tell, with exactitude and craft. To the melting love in my stomach was added a sudden ache, and with an involuntary motion that was quite inexplicable (for one brought up to mind where he put his hands) I gently grasped her wrist, looking more closely at the tattoo. Even at that instant I knew my curiosity might be offensive, but I couldn't help myself.

"Where were you?" I said.

She spoke a fibrous name in Polish, which I understood, barely, to be "Oświeçim." Then she said, "I was there for a long time."

As she went slowly up the stairs I took a good look at her body in its clinging silk summer dress. While it was a beautiful body, with all the right prominences, curves, continuities and symmetries, there was something a little strange about it— nothing visibly missing and not so much deficient as reassembled. And that was precisely *it*, I could see. The odd quality proclaimed itself through the skin. It possessed the sickish plasticity (at the back of her arms it was especially noticeable) of one who has suffered severe emaciation and whose flesh is even now in the last stages of being restored. Also, I felt that underneath that healthy suntan there lingered the sallowness of a body not wholly rescued from a terrible crisis. But none of these at all diminished a kind of wonderfully negligent sexuality having to do at that moment, at least, with the casual but forthright way her pelvis moved and with her truly sumptuous rear end. Despite past famine, her behind was as perfectly formed as some fantastic prize-winning pear; it vibrated with magical eloquence, and from this angle it so stirred my depths that I mentally pledged to the Presbyterian orphanages of Virginia a quarter of my future earnings as a writer in exchange for that bare ass's brief lodging—thirty seconds would do—within the compass of my cupped, supplicant palms. Old Stingo, I mused as she climbed upward, there must be some perversity in this dorsal fixation. Then as she reached the top of the stairs she turned, looking down, and smiled the saddest smile imaginable. "I hope I haven't annoyed you with my problems," she said. "I am so sorry." And she moved toward her room and said, "Good night."

*Did you read a lot of survivor literature?*

I read a certain amount. The odd thing about the Holocaust is that there is a sameness to the accounts, which prevents one from having to read a vast number. There was also a kind of ultimate horror. Once you have absorbed a few of the details, you don't need to absorb a great deal more.

*There is a view that says, first, that only survivors should attempt to recreate the Holocaust in literature or film; and second, that any attempt to recreate it necessarily diminishes the event. Were you worried about any of that as you wrote?*

No. Of course, I was perfectly aware of the argument in favour of silence, and also the argument that says that anyone who is not a survivor is incapable of rendering the story. I simply don't agree with either of those points of view. I realized I was treading on very delicate ground, and I did not want to rush into it in any haphazard way. I knew there was a risk, but at the same time I balked at the idea that, as horrible as it was, the Holocaust was some sort of sacrosanct area that could not be treated. I especially balked at the idea that someone who was not there was incapable of dealing with it. If that is true, then it is true for all experience. It would have prevented our greatest Civil War novel from having been written. *The Red Badge of Courage* was written by Stephen Crane, a man who was never within a hundred miles of a battlefield, and yet it remains our most powerful document about the combat side of civil war.

Until I read this passage I had rather simple-mindedly thought that only I had entertained such speculation, that only *I* had become obsessed about the time relation—to the extent, for example, that I had attempted more or less successfully to pinpoint my own activities on the first day of April, 1943, the day when Sophie, entering Auschwitz, fell into the "slow hands of the living damnation." At some point late in 1947—only a relatively brief number of years removed from the beginning of Sophie's ordeal—I rummaged through my memory in an attempt to locate myself in time on the same day that Sophie walked through the gates of hell. The first day of April, 1943— April Fools' Day—had a mnemonic urgency for me, and after going through some of my father's letters to me, which handily corroborated my movements, I was able to come up with the absurd fact that on that afternoon, as Sophie first set foot on the railroad platform in Auschwitz, it was a lovely spring morning in Raleigh, North Carolina, where I was gorging myself on bananas. I was eating myself nearly sick with bananas, the reason being that in the coming hour I was to take a physical examination for entrance into the Marine Corps. At the age of seventeen, already over six feet tall but weighing only 122 pounds, I knew I had to put on three more pounds to satisfy the minimum weight requirement. Stomach grossly bulging like that of a starveling, naked on a set of scales in front of a brawny old recruiting sergeant who stared at my emaciated adolescent beanpole of a frame and uttered a sneering "Je*sus* Christ" (there was also a snotty joke about April Fools' Day), I squeaked past by scant ounces.

On that day I had not heard of Auschwitz, nor of any concentration camp, nor of the mass destruction of the European Jews, nor even much about the Nazis. For me the enemy in that global war was the Japanese, and my ignorance of the anguish hovering like a noxious gray smog over places with names like Auschwitz, Treblinka, Bergen-Belsen was complete. But wasn't this true for most Americans, indeed most human beings who dwelt beyond the perimeter of the Nazi horror? "This notion of different orders of time simultaneous but in no effective analogy or communication," Steiner continues, "may be necessary to the rest of us, who were not there, who lived as if on another planet." Quite so—especially when (and the fact is often forgotten) for millions of Americans the embodiment of evil during that time was not the Nazis, despised and feared as they were, but the legions of Japanese soldiers who swarmed the jungles of the Pacific like astigmatic and rabid little apes and whose threat to the American mainland seemed far more dangerous, not to say more repulsive, given their yellowness and their filthy habits. But even if such narrowly focused animosity against an Oriental foe had not been real, most people could scarcely have known about the Nazi death camps, and this makes Steiner's ruminations all the more instructive. The nexus between these "different orders of time" is, of course—for those of us who were not there—someone who *was* there, and this brings me back to Sophie. To Sophie and, in particular, to Sophie's relation with SS Obersturmbannführer Rudolf Franz Höss.

I have spoken several times about Sophie's reticence concerning Auschwitz, her firm and generally unyielding silence about that fetid sinkhole of her past. Since she herself (as she once admitted to me) had so successfully anesthetized her mind against recurring images of her encampment in the abyss, it is small wonder that neither Nathan nor I ever gained much knowledge of what happened to her on a *day-to-day* basis (especially during the last months) aside from the quite obvious fact that she had come close to death from malnutrition and more than one contagion. Thus the jaded reader surfeited with our century's perdurable feast of atrocities will be spared here a detailed chronicle of the killings, gassings, beatings, tortures, criminal medical experiments, slow deprivations, excremental outrages, screaming madnesses and other entries into the historical account which have already been made by Tadeusz Borowski, Jean-François Steiner, Olga Lengyel, Eugen Kogon,

André Schwarz-Bart, Elie Wiesel and Bruno Bettelheim, to name but a few of the most eloquent who have tried to limn the totally infernal in their heart's blood. My vision of Sophie's stay at Auschwitz is necessarily particularized, and perhaps a little distorted, though honestly so. Even if she had decided to reveal either to Nathan or me the gruesome minutiae of her twenty months at Auschwitz, I might be constrained to draw down the veil, for, as George Steiner remarks, it is not clear "that those who were not themselves fully involved should touch upon these agonies unscathed." I have been haunted, I must confess, by an element of presumption in the sense of being an intruder upon the terrain of an experience so bestial, so inexplicable, so undetachably and rightfully the possession alone of those who suffered and died, or survived it. A survivor, Elie Wiesel, has written: "Novelists made free use of [the Holocaust] in their work . . . In so doing they cheapened [it], drained it of its substance. The Holocaust was now a hot topic, fashionable, guaranteed to gain attention and to achieve instant success . . ." I do not know how ultimately valid any of this is, but I am aware of the risk.

Yet I cannot accept Steiner's suggestion that *silence* is the answer, that it is best "not to add the trivia of literary, sociological debate to the unspeakable." Nor do I agree with the idea that "in the presence of certain realities art is trivial or impertinent." I find a touch of piety in this, especially inasmuch as Steiner has not remained silent. And surely, almost cosmic in its incomprehensibility as it may appear, the embodiment of evil which Auschwitz has become remains impenetrable only so long as we shrink from trying to penetrate it, however inadequately; and Steiner himself adds immediately that the *next* best is "to try and understand." I have thought that it might be possible to make a stab at understanding Auschwitz by trying to understand Sophie, who to say the least was a cluster of contradictions. Although she was not Jewish, she had suffered as much as any Jew who had survived the same afflictions, and—as I think will be made plain—had in certain profound ways suffered more than most. (It is surpassingly difficult for many Jews to see beyond the consecrated nature of the Nazis' genocidal fury, and thus it seems to me less a flaw than a pardonable void in the moving meditation of Steiner, a

Jew, that he makes only fleeting reference to the vast multitudes of non-Jews—the myriad Slavs and the Gypsies—who were swallowed up in the apparatus of the camps, perishing just as surely as the Jews, though sometimes only less methodically.) If Sophie had been just a victim—helpless as a blown leaf, a human speck, volitionless, like so many multitudes of her fellow damned—she would have seemed merely pathetic, another wretched waif of the storm cast up in Brooklyn with no secrets which had to be unlocked. But the fact of the matter is that at Auschwitz (and this she came gradually to confess to me that summer) she had been a victim, yes, but both victim and accomplice, accessory—however haphazard and ambiguous and uncalculating her design—to the mass slaughter whose sickening vaporous residue spiraled skyward from the chimneys of Birkenau whenever she peered out across the parched autumnal meadows from the windows of the mansard roof of the house of her captor, Rudolf Höss. And therein lay one (although not the only one) of the prime causes of her devastating guilt—the guilt she concealed from Nathan and which, with no inkling of its nature or its actuality, he so often cruelly inflamed. For she could not wriggle out from beneath the suffocating knowledge that there had been this time in her life when she had played out the role, to its limit, of a fellow conspirator in crime. And this was the role of an obsessed and poisonous anti-Semite—a passionate, avid, tediously single-minded hater of Jews.

*Elie Wiesel and his colleagues would presumably argue that the enormity of Auschwitz and of the Holocaust was qualitatively different. Against it, even evocations of the Civil War are diminished.*

I certainly understand that aspect of the argument. And for that reason, I approached the subject with as much humility as I could muster. I realized that I was dealing with something totally unusual, not an ordinary catastrophe, but an exceptional catastrophe of universal scope. Even so, I could not be persuaded that this should prevent someone from dealing with it.

*Did you deal with it because of the creative impulse of the novelist, or because you wanted the world to understand what had happened and what the implications were?*

Some of both, I think. I don't know which component loomed the largest in my reckoning when I started the book. I was haunted by the central metaphor, which is the choice. In the book I mentioned, *Five Chimneys*, the author, Dr. Olga Lengyel, did not have to make the choice that Sophie had to make, but she did lose her two children because of a miscalculation. She was trying to protect them, but she made a miscalculation. I can't remember exactly, but I think she said that one of the children was younger or older; at any rate, they both went to the gas chamber. That demonstrated to me the unbelievable, haphazard horror of the Nazi tyranny. Then in the 1960s I read Hannah Arendt's book, *Eichmann in Jerusalem*. Somewhere in the text, she mentions, in passing, a gypsy woman who was forced to make that choice, in other words to become the murderer of one of her children. That struck me between the eyes, and I made the link between Olga Lengyel and that woman. I suddenly realized that this had to be the metaphor for the most horrible, tyrannical despotism in history, that this was a new form of evil, an evil so total that it could cause a woman to murder one of her own children. That was the central guiding, motivating factor behind writing *Sophie's Choice*.

She and the children were undergoing at this very moment the ordeal she had heard about—rumored in Warsaw a score of times in whispers—but which had seemed at once so unbearable and unlikely to happen to her that she had thrust it out of her mind. But here she was, and here was the doctor. While over there—just beyond the roofs of the boxcars recently vacated by the death-bound Malkinia Jews—was Birkenau, and the doctor could select for its abyssal doors anyone whom he desired. This thought caused her such terror that instead of keeping her mouth shut she said, *"Ich bin polnisch! In Krakow geboren!"* Then she blurted helplessly, "I'm not Jewish! Or my children—they're not Jewish either." And added, "They are racially pure. They speak German." Finally she announced, "I'm a Christian. I'm a devout Catholic."

The doctor turned again. His eyebrows arched and he looked at Sophie with inebriate, wet, fugitive eyes, unsmiling. He was now so close to her that she smelled plainly the alcoholic vapor—a rancid fragrance of barley or rye—and she was not strong enough to return his gaze. It was then that she knew she had said something wrong, perhaps fatally wrong. She averted her face for an instant, glancing at an adjoining line of prisoners shambling through the golgotha of their selection, and saw Eva's flute teacher Zaorski at the precise congealed instant of his doom—dispatched to the left and to Birkenau by an almost imperceptible nod of a doctor's head. Now, turning back, she heard Dr. Jemand von Niemand say, "So you're not a Communist. You're a believer."

"*Ja, mein Hauptmann.* I believe in Christ." What folly! She sensed from his manner, his gaze—the new look in his eye of luminous intensity—that everything she was saying, far from helping her, from protecting her, was leading somehow to her swift undoing. She thought: Let me be struck dumb.

The doctor was a little unsteady on his feet. He leaned over for a moment to an enlisted underling with a clipboard and murmured something, meanwhile absorbedly picking his nose. Eva, pressing heavily against Sophie's leg, began to cry. "So you believe in Christ the Redeemer?" the doctor said in a thick-tongued but oddly abstract voice, like that of a lecturer examining the delicately shaded facet of a proposition in logic. Then he said something which for an instant was totally mystifying: "Did He not say, 'Suffer the little children to come unto Me'?" He turned back to her, moving with the twitchy methodicalness of a drunk.

Sophie, with an inanity poised on her tongue and choked with fear, was about to attempt a reply when the doctor said, "You may keep one of your children."

"*Bitte?*" said Sophie.

"You may keep one of your children," he repeated. "The other one will have to go. Which one will you keep?"

"You mean, I have to choose?"

"You're a Polack, not a Yid. That gives you a privilege—a choice."

Her thought processes dwindled, ceased. Then she felt her legs crumple. "I can't choose! I can't choose!" She began to scream. Oh, how she recalled her own screams! Tormented angels never screeched so loudly above hell's pandemonium. *"Ich kann nicht wählen!"* she screamed.

The doctor was aware of unwanted attention. "Shut up!" he ordered. "Hurry now and choose. Choose, goddamnit, or I'll send them both over there. Quick!"

She could not believe any of this. She could not believe that she was now kneeling on the hurtful, abrading concrete, drawing her children toward her so smotheringly tight that she felt that their flesh might be engrafted to hers even through layers of clothes. Her disbelief was total, deranged. It was disbelief reflected in the eyes of the gaunt, waxy-skinned young Rottenführer, the doctor's aide, to whom she inexplicably found herself looking upward in supplication. He appeared stunned, and he returned her gaze with a wide-eyed baffled expression, as if to say: I can't understand this either.

"Don't make me choose," she heard herself plead in a whisper, "I can't choose."

"Send them both over there, then," the doctor said to the aide, *"nach links."*

"Mama!" She heard Eva's thin but soaring cry at the instant that she thrust the child away from her and rose from the concrete with a clumsy stumbling motion. "Take the baby!" she called out. "Take my little girl!"

At this point the aide—with a careful gentleness that Sophie would try without success to forget—tugged at Eva's hand and led her away into the waiting legion of the damned. She would forever retain a dim impression that the child had continued to look back, beseeching. But because she was now almost completely blinded by salty, thick, copious tears she was spared whatever expression Eva wore, and she was always grateful for that. For in the bleakest honesty of her heart she knew that she would never have been able to tolerate it, driven nearly mad as she was by her last glimpse of that vanishing small form.

"She still had her *mis*—and her flute," Sophie said as she finished talking to me. "All these years I have never been able to bear those words. Or bear to speak them, in any language."

*Yet the question of choice was endemic to the entire Holocaust experience. It was not unusual. It was true of all ghetto life, all the deportations. Families were often given only three meal tickets for five, and they had to choose who would live and who would die within the family structure. Kids were constantly being separated that way. But I take it that it was so visceral for you that it seemed to sum up the evil incarnate?*

Yes, it's almost a poetic metaphor, in a gruesome way. It summed up the absolute totalitarian nature of this evil, which we really had not seen, certainly in civilized society, since history began to be recorded. It seized me so poignantly that I was compelled to write a book about it. I also connected it with something that had happened to me: I went to Brooklyn, in the late 1940s, and met a young—older than I was, but nonetheless young—woman who had been a survivor of Auschwitz, and who had a tattoo on her arm. Her name was Sophie.

*Was she Polish and Catholic?*

She was Polish and Catholic. Oddly enough, I got a letter not too long ago from a woman who had been in that same house at roughly the same time. She reminded me that Sophie looked a bit like Ursula Andress, which indeed she did.

*In your essay, "Hell Reconsidered," you express the view that the world must know that the Holocaust was not merely a Jewish phenomenon, but that it embraced many others.*

People like Ele Wiesel have resisted this idea, with some justification, I think, because of the way it has been presented to the world. I don't think for an instant that anyone can object to the fact that Jews, quite properly, say that they were the chief victims. Indeed they were; there is simply no doubt about it. In fact, I think it can be argued that the phrase "the war against the Jews" describes what the Nazis were doing to a great extent. It was an overriding obsession.

*Wiesel said, "Not all victims were Jews, but all Jews were victims."*

Yes, I think that is true. But I am troubled nonetheless by a certain ungenerosity that does not allow the understanding that there were, indeed, not just thousands, not hundreds of thousands, but millions of non-Jews who died just as horribly as the Jews, although perhaps not as methodically. It has to be remembered that the population of Auschwitz at any single time was largely Gentile, not Jewish. The Jewish victims were being exterminated, to be sure, and the non-Jews were dying in their own particular way, which is to say that they were slaves who were being starved to death, and they died just as verifiably as those who went to the gas chamber. This has bothered me; it has bothered even people like Simon Wiesenthal, the leading Nazi hunter of our era. He is on record as saying that he is troubled by the fact that "the six million" seems to be proprietary. He says, "I always insist that we talk about not the six million Jews but the ten million, or the eleven million or whatever number of people, Jews and non-Jews, who were direct victims of the Nazi terror." I think that there should be a kind of codicil or postscript or some banner floating along with the Jewish banner, saying, "We also died."

*Is Sophie your codicil?*

In a sense. I certainly didn't write the book to make a message. To be quite honest I have been very moved by the reaction on the part of so many Jews who accept Sophie for what she was, and who also accept the fact that the book never fails to demonstrate that the Jews were the chief victims and that Sophie's own father, who was a rabid anti-Semite, was a necessary instrument for this horror. I have tried to use

Sophie not in any sort of agit-prop way to say that others died, but to demonstrate quietly that there were more than a few Poles who were caught in the same sort of agony as the Jews.

*I did an interview recently with Yaffa Eliach, who has written a book,* Hasidic Tales of the Holocaust. *And when I questioned her about Sophie, she asked how many Polish Catholics stood on that platform at Auschwitz and had to make that choice, compared to the vast numbers of Jewish mothers who stood on that same platform.*

If one wishes to speak numerically, no one could ever argue with the fact that the Jews were the chief recipients of the horror. I don't think there is any argument about that. But it seems to me if one Polish child suffers direct agony at the hands of the Nazis, this is an indication of what the Nazis were up to. It wasn't just one little Polish child: there were literally hundreds of thousands, even millions of Slavs who suffered. To be sure, they did not suffer the direct extermination process, but they died horribly of disease, torture, starvation, medical experiments, and so on. My point is quite simple: they should be put somewhere into the record.

*What did you think of the film of your book?*

I thought the film was a remarkably faithful adaptation of the book. I thought it did a splendid job, in a linear way, of representing the book. At the same time, the film necessarily had to commit rather enormous sins of omission, and much of the book was not in the film. I regretted that, but that is implicit in the making of movies. It would have been a ten- or twelve-hour movie if it had tried to reproduce the complexity of the book.

*In failing to reproduce the complexity of the book, does it do the subject-matter an injustice?*

No, I don't think so. I think that the great virtue of the film is that it extracted the essence of the book, the central story. The message of the book was retained. Of course, it could not contain any of the purely philosophical points that were made, but I thought it did an awfully good job of capturing the basic outline.

*You did? I thought it was a betrayal of your book, if I may be direct about it. I felt that the inability to convey what Auschwitz was, what those seething platforms were, what the crematoria were, constituted a betrayal. Apart from all of that, I thought: here's a writer who has intellectually and aesthetically established the nature of the evil and along comes a film crew and violates it.*

Well, I certainly had no feeling of happiness over what the film failed to do. There were so many vast areas of the book that were not even suggested. I sensed a terrible sort of emptiness in myself after I had seen the film. But my feeling of deeply qualified approval does have to do with the fact that I thought it caught the essence of Sophie's horror, of Sophie's agony. And did it rather well through the extraordinary performance of Meryl Streep. Knowing the films as I do, I think it could have been totally parodied, totally ruined, but I don't think it ruined the book.

*You talked of* Holocaust, *the TV series, in your essay "Hell Reconsidered." You called it soft-headed vulgarity and slick footage. But you would feel, I take it, that even a film that ultimately trivializes the event is better than no film at all.*

I would say so. Naturally it is difficult to be objective about the difference between the movie of *Sophie's Choice* and a television programme like *Holocaust*. But despite my lack of objectivity, I think I would have to say that the movie of *Sophie* is a far more honest attempt to capture the essence of the Holocaust than the television series was. I felt that there was a severe dishonesty in the television series, but I did not feel that there was any dishonesty in Pakula's approach to the film. I felt it failed on many levels, but that if there was honesty in the book, he replicated that honesty to some degree. Therefore, to answer your question, yes, I feel it is better to have a frail and faulty version than to have nothing at all. Despite the caveats you've just mentioned, there have been a lot of people who probably would not read the book but who leave the movie feeling that they had learned something or were moved in some way.

*Does it concern you that for the lumpen proletariat* Sophie's Choice *is the Holocaust? It is the single most vivid evocation that society has embraced in a combination of literature and film in recent memory. Therefore, isn't it a little worrisome that the book has so much greater fidelity than the film?*

You're right. One could possibly be left with the impression, if one were unsophisticated, that the film is the Holocaust. The book explains in much greater detail that the Holocaust was far more complex.

*You achieve, in the book, an extraordinary combination of fact and art, if you will forgive the separation. You use Höss's material. You use Steiner's. You use established works to give authenticity and an intellectual frame. Was that a difficult process?*

For me it wasn't so much difficult as necessary. I felt that I had to draw upon what insights had been provided by people much more knowledgeable than I about the period. I felt that I had to do my homework. I wanted to be as absolutely accurate as I could about my facts and figures, and I've been pleased that I've had almost no major objections from people who might be expected to make objections, scholars of the period and so on. This is not to say that I wanted in any sense to over-research the book. I think books that are overly researched smell of the library and, therefore, don't work. So I was very careful. I read, I think, just enough. I read Steiner, I read Hanna Arendt. I read survivors' documents. But I imagine the total number of hours I spent in reading was very modest.

*D.M. Thomas also went back to one survivor's account to give authenticity that couldn't be achieved, he felt, by interposed description.*

Yes, I think that that was very wise. One has to obey one's instincts if one is writing a novel; it's a mysterious process, but you have to obey your gut feeling rather than your head sometimes.

*There is in your book, as in Thomas's, a lot of sexuality, some would say eroticism.*

Given the nature of the relationship between Sophie and Nathan, I think I would have been remiss had I not tried to explore the sado-masochistic eroticism that existed. Sophie and Nathan were possessed by some sort of demons that caused them to devour each other, and that involved a great deal of erotic lunacy. After all, they did kill each other, and they had to come very close to the brink. As a metaphor, death and love have always been entwined in literature. The death wish and the procreative wish have often been so closely connected you can't separate them. That was essential to me, and to the relationship between Sophie and Nathan. I might add, parenthetically, that it is one of the things that I think was totally lost in the movie. There was some sort of timidity, almost, which prevented the movie from touching on that very important area of the relationship between Sophie and Nathan. It vitiated the whole ending, to my mind, because there is no premonition, as you get in the book, of why and how they're going to die together, by mutual suicide, by poisoning, not even a hint of that in the movie.

*The Holocaust theme is a theme of such darkness that, in those books that deal with it, the sexual relationships are bleak and self-destructive and almost pornographic themselves, as though in some wretched way they were a mirror of the event.*

You are making a connection between the quasi-pornographic, almost brutal sexuality and the pornography of violence, which, of course, was rampant at Auschwitz. And I think that, possibly consciously or unconsciously, in trying to outline the sexual connection between Sophie and Nathan, and the violence of it, I was indeed trying to connect it to the brutality of Auschwitz. I mean, after all, he kicks her, breaks her rib, he urinates on her. This was a mirror of the kind of the thing that was going on at Auschwitz daily.

*Has the book yet been translated?*

It has been translated into, I think, twenty-two languages. In France, it is now the best-known serious American novel since World War Two.

*Do you get different responses from different cultures?*

In a curious way, it's the little things that interest me. For instance, I've not been allowed to be published in Poland—largely because of the fact that I bear down fairly heavily on Polish anti-Semitism. Some of the Polish actors, when the movie was being made in Yugoslavia, were warned officially that they could not come back to Poland if they played in the movie. In the Soviet Union, part of the book has been translated, to great fanfare, but they've put an official block on it for some reason. And it has been published in Hebrew, and I've received quite a few letters from Israel about the book, all of them favourable. The summer before last, I received a rather wonderful telephone call from Tel Aviv from a woman who just wanted to say how much she liked it.

*It's immensely gratifying as a writer, isn't it, when those spontaneous things happen?*

Yes, that makes one feel very good.

*One last question. Your works all deal with individual suffering in historical terms—what might be termed the continuing slavery of humankind.*

Yes. A form of human domination seems to be a constant in human history. Part of the message, if there is such a thing as a message, in *Sophie's Choice* was that the Nazis actually got everyone. They got the Jews first and foremost and most specifically, but anything so deadly, anything so utterly consummately filled with evil has to have at least a residual effect on everyone else. This seems to me the chief weakness of the totally proprietary notion of the Holocaust by Jews. Just the magnitude of the venture had to cause suffering that was universal.

# Further Reading

## Selected works by authors interviewed:

**Appelfeld, Aharon**. *The Age of Wonders*. Trans. Dalya Bilu. Toronto: Lester & Orpen Dennys, 1982.

**Appelfeld, Aharon**. *Badenheim 1939*. Trans. Dalya Bilu. Boston: David R. Godine, 1980.

**Appelfeld, Aharon**. *Tzili*. Trans. Dalya Bilu. New York: E.P. Dutton, 1983.

**Becker, Jurek**. *Jacob the Liar*. Trans. Melvin Kornfeld. New York: Harcourt Brace Jovanovich, 1975.

**Eliach, Yaffa**. *Hasidic Tales of the Holocaust*. New York: Oxford University Press, 1982. Also available in paperback.

**Insdorf, Annette**. *Indelible Shadows: Film and the Holocaust*. New York: Random House, 1983.

**Steiner, George**. *Language and Silence: Essays on Language, Literature and the Inhuman*. New York: Atheneum, 1967.

**Steiner, George**. *The Portage to San Cristòbal of A.H.* London: Faber and Faber, 1981. Also available in paperback.

**Styron, William**. *Sophie's Choice*. New York: Random House, 1979. Also available in paperback.

**Styron, William**. *This Quiet Dust and Other Writings*. New York: Random House, 1982.

**Syberberg, Hans Jürgen**. *The Films of Hans Jürgen Syberberg*. Trans. Peter Green. London: The Goethe Institute, n.d.

**Syberberg, Hans Jürgen**. *The New German Cinema*. John Sandford. London: Oswald Wolff, p. 116 ff.

**Thomas, D.M.** *The White Hotel*. London: Victor Gollancz, 1981. Also available in paperback.

Wiesel, Elie. *Night*. Trans. Stella Rodway. New York: Farrar, Straus & Giroux, 1980.


## Selected fiction, poems and drama by other authors:

Borowski, Tadeusz. *This Way for the Gas, Ladies and Gentlemen*. New York: Viking, 1967.

Hersey, John. *The Wall*. New York: Knopf, 1950.

Hochhuth, Rolf. *The Deputy*. New York: Grove Press, 1964.

*I Never Saw Another Butterfly*. New York: McGraw-Hill, 1964.

Jackson, Livia E. Bitton. *Elli: Coming of Age in the Holocaust*. Toronto: Fitzhenry & Whiteside, 1983.

Jacot, Michael. *The Last Butterfly*. Indianapolis: Bobbs-Merrill, 1974.

Korn, Rachel. *Generation: Selected Poems*. Oakville: Mosaic Press/Valley Editions, 1983.

Kosinski, Jerzy. *The Painted Bird*. New York: Pocket Books, 1966.

Kovner, Abba and Nelly Sachs. *Selected Poems*. London: Penguin Books, 1971.

Oberski, Jona. *A Childhood: A Novella*. Trans. Ralph Manheim. Toronto: Lester & Orpen Dennys, 1983.

Sachs, Nelly. *O The Chimneys*. New York: Farrar, Straus & Giroux, 1967.

Schaefer, Susan Fromberg. *Anya*. New York: Macmillan, 1974.

Schwarz-Bart, André. *The Last of the Just*. New York: Atheneum, 1961.

# Works for further reference:

**Bettelheim, Bruno.** *The Informed Heart: Autonomy in a Mass Age.* New York: Avon, 1971.

**Chartock, Roselle and Jack Spencer.** *The Holocaust Years: Society on Trial.* New York: Bantam, 1978.

**Conot, Robert.** *Justice at Nuremberg: the First Comprehensive Dramatic Account of the Trial of the Leaders.* New York: Harper and Row, 1983.

**Dawidowicz, Lucy S.** *The War Against the Jews, 1933-1945.* New York: Holt, Rinehart and Winston, 1975.

**Fackenheim, Emil L.** *The Jewish Return into History: Reflections in the Age of Auschwitz & a New Jerusalem.* New York: Schocken, 1978.

**Harris, Frederick J.** *Encounters with Darkness: French and German Writers on World War II.* New York: Oxford University Press, 1983.

**Hilberg, Raul.** *The Destruction of European Jewry.* Chicago: Quadrangle, 1967.

**Kaplan, Chaim A.** *Scroll of Agony: The Warsaw Diary of Chaim A. Kaplan.* Ed. Abraham Katch. New York: Macmillan, 1981.

**Langer, Lawrence L.** *The Holocaust and the Literary Imagination.* Princeton: Yale University Press, 1975.

**Laqueur, Walter.** *The Terrible Secret.* Boston: Little, Brown, 1980.

*Voices from the Holocaust.* Ed. Sylvia Rothchild. New York: New American Library, 1981.

**von Lang, Jochen.** *Eichmann Interrogated: Transcripts from the Archives of the Israeli Police.* Trans. Ralph Manheim. Toronto: Lester & Orpen Dennys, 1983.

**Ziemian, Joseph.** *The Cigarette Sellers of Three Crosses Square.* Trans. Janina David. Lerner, 1970.

# About Stephen Lewis

Stephen Lewis was born in Ottawa in 1937. After attending the Universities of Toronto and British Columbia, Lewis taught and travelled in Africa before returning to Canada to work for the New Democratic Party. At the age of twenty-five, he was elected to the Ontario Legislature. He became Ontario NDP leader in 1970 and Leader of the Opposition in 1975.

Since resigning from politics in 1978, Lewis has lectured widely in Canada and the United States on subjects ranging from contemporary affairs to children's literature. He sits regularly on labour arbitration boards, and is a consultant to various public-interest groups. In recognition of his work in the fields of public-policy development and humanitarian concerns he has been awarded a Doctor of Laws from McMaster University and is a Fellow of Ryerson Polytechnical Institute. His daily radio and television commentaries on political and social issues earned for him the 1982 Gordon Sinclair ACTRA Award for outspoken opinion and integrity in broadcasting.

Stephen Lewis is married to *Toronto Star* columnist Michele Landsberg. They have three children.